New Mexico is full of rustic hot springs like this one at Jemez Hot Springs.

TOURING
HOT SPRINGS
NEW MEXICO

Withdrawn ABCL

The State's Best Resorts and Rustic Soaks

THIRD EDITION

Matt C. Bischoff

FALCONGUIDES

GUILFORD, CONNECTICUT

FALCONGUIDES®

An imprint of The Rowman & Littlefield Publishing Group, Inc.
4501 Forbes Blvd., Ste. 200
Lanham, MD 20706
www.rowman.com

Falcon and FalconGuides are registered trademarks and Make Adventure Your
Story is a trademark of The Rowman & Littlefield Publishing Group, Inc.

Distributed by NATIONAL BOOK NETWORK

Photos by Matt C. Bischoff

Maps by Melissa Baker

British Library Cataloguing in Publication Information available

Library of Congress Cataloging-in-Publication Data available

ISBN 978-1-4930-4241-8 (paperback)
ISBN 978-1-4930-4242-5 (e-book)

∞™ The paper used in this publication meets the minimum requirements of
American National Standard for Information Sciences—Permanence of Paper for
Printed Library Materials, ANSI/NISO Z39.48-1992.

CONTENTS

Introduction ix

    Hot Springs in History ix

    Therapeutic Aspects xi

    Geology of Hot Springs xi

How to Use This Book xv

    Book Organization xv

    How to Find the Hot Springs xvi

Precautions xvii

Responsible Behavior xix

Author's Favorites xx

The Hot Springs

SOUTHERN NEW MEXICO

San Francisco River Area 2

    1. San Francisco Hot Springs 3

    2. Sundial Springs 7

    3. Frisco Box Hot Springs 9

    4. Faywood Hot Springs 13

Gila Hot Springs and the Gila Wilderness Area 16

    5. Melanie Hot Springs 18

    6. Gila Hot Springs 21

    7. Wildwood Retreat and Hot Springs 23

    8. The Wilderness Lodge 25

    9. Gila Hot Springs RV Park and Campground 27

    10. Middle Fork (Lightfeather) Hot Springs 28

    11. Jordan Hot Springs 31

    12. The Meadows Warm Springs 35

    13. Turkey Creek Hot Springs 37

    14. Brock Canyon Hot Springs 41

Rio Grande Region 44

    15. Radium Springs 46

    16. Riverbend Hot Springs 50

17. Charles Motel and Spa 53

18. Fire Water Lodge 55

19. La Paloma Too Hot Springs (Hay-Yo-Kay Hot Springs) 57

20. Indian Springs 59

21. La Paloma Hot Springs & Spa 61

22. Artesian Bath House and RV Park 63

23. Pelican Spa 64

24. Sierra Grande 66

25. Hoosier Hot Springs 68

26. Blackstone Hotsprings 69

NORTHERN NEW MEXICO

Jemez Springs Area (Santa Fe National Forest) 72

27. Spence Hot Springs 73

28. McCauley Hot Springs 76

29. San Antonio Hot Springs 78

30. Soda Dam 81

31. Jemez Springs Bath House 83

32. Jemez Hot Springs (Giggling Springs) 86

Santa Fe Area 89

33. Ten Thousand Waves 90

34. Montezuma Hot Springs 93

Taos Area 96

35. Black Rock Hot Springs 97

36. Manby Hot Springs 100

37. Ojo Caliente Mineral Springs Resort & Spa 104

38. Ponce de Leon Hot Springs
    (Taos Pueblo Tribal Hot Springs) 107

Appendix A: Further Reading 110

Appendix B: For More Information 111

Index 114

About the Author 115

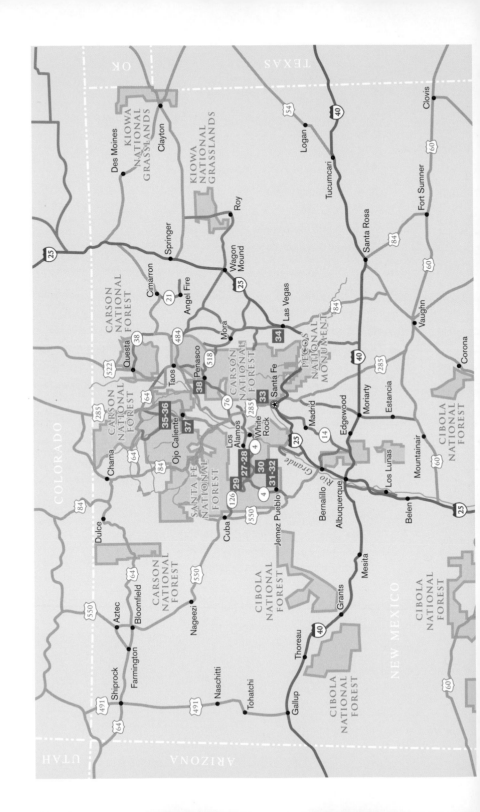

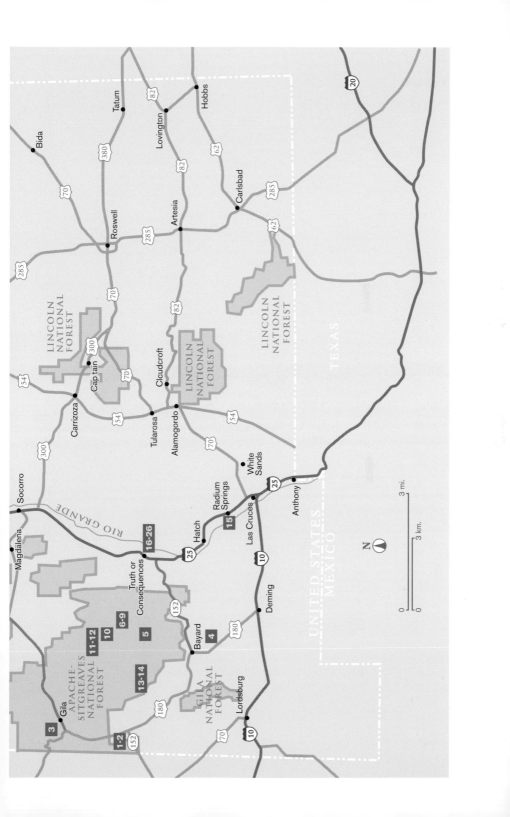

Map Legend

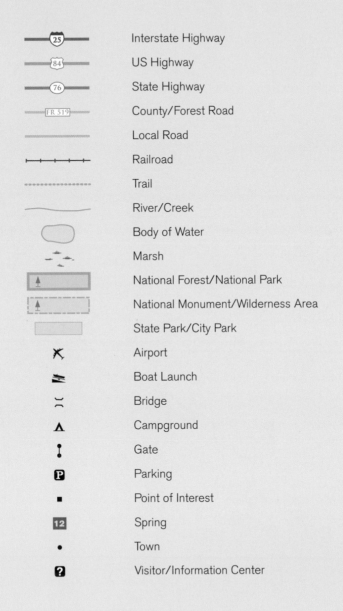

══(25)══	Interstate Highway
══(84)══	US Highway
══(76)══	State Highway
══FR 519══	County/Forest Road
═══════	Local Road
┝┿┿┿┿┥	Railroad
▪▪▪▪▪▪▪▪	Trail
⌇⌇⌇	River/Creek
⬭	Body of Water
⌁⌁	Marsh
▮	National Forest/National Park
▯	National Monument/Wilderness Area
▢	State Park/City Park
✕	Airport
⬎	Boat Launch
⏝	Bridge
Λ	Campground
!	Gate
P	Parking
▪	Point of Interest
12	Spring
•	Town
?	Visitor/Information Center

INTRODUCTION

HOT SPRINGS IN HISTORY

Hot springs have held a central place in numerous cultures throughout time. Prehistorically, hot springs were used for bathing and food preparation, and likely held spiritual meaning to many diverse groups. According to archaeological evidence, balneology—the utilization of natural mineral waters for the treatment of disease—has been practiced for more than 5,000 years. Hot springs have been used in religious rites and ceremonies in both Egypt and the Middle East for thousands of years.

Hot Springs in Europe

According to English legend, Prince Bladud (who was to become the father of King Lear) contracted leprosy at a young age and was banished from his father's kingdom. Forced to eke a living from herding swine, the pigs themselves contracted the prince's disease. As the legend goes, one day the pigs were wallowing in hot spring water on the banks of a river and miraculously emerged cured of their disease. Noticing this, the young prince also bathed in the water and also miraculously emerged healed. The story of this incredible cure spread rapidly, and the hot spring waters became a popular place to visit. Today we know the site as Bath, England.

Several centuries following Prince Bladud, Roman soldiers visited the site and recuperated from their long campaigns in the hot spring water. Word of the springs spread across the Roman Empire, and Bath quickly developed as a resort town. Through the centuries people continued to believe in the curative powers of the waters at Bath. The Royal Mineral Water Hospital was established at Bath by the British parliament in 1739 and evolved into a therapeutic treatment center for a variety of ailments.

The Victorian era in Europe saw a great awakening in the interest in spas and hot spring waters, particularly in the medicinal benefits attributed to drinking the waters, although bathing was still an important activity. A visit to a spa became a fashionable pastime for Europe's wealthy, and centers of thermal waters that had earlier been exploited by the Romans were developed into elaborate resort-hotel complexes.

Hot Springs in America

In the mid-nineteenth century, the popularity of hot spring resorts spread from Europe to America. Berkeley Springs in West Virginia, one of the earliest popular spas in North America, was originally named Bath in honor of the spa in England. Like most hot springs in North America, Native Americans had used the Berkeley Springs long before the arrival of Europeans; various tribes used the springs as a kind of neutral ground, where peaceful meetings could be held. The British colonials themselves used Berkeley Springs as meeting places, and continued to believe in their therapeutic value.

New hot springs were "discovered" as the American people began moving west, and by 1888 there were 8,843 springs recorded in the United States. Of these springs, 634 were spas and 223 were sources of commercial mineral water for consumption. Hot spring popularity was particularly pronounced from the 1880s through the turn of the century. For years people had used the natural hot spring pools and ponds for therapy, but the Victorians desired a more civilized way of bathing. Resorts and spas became the answer, allowing for private and controlled bathing in the medicinal waters. Because of the lower population and lack of governmental support in America, however, these springs never became as extensive as their European counterparts.

The heyday for the establishment of spas and resorts at hot springs in the United States occurred in the early twentieth century, and countless hot springs throughout the country attest to this boom time in commercial hot spring bathing. These resorts generally promised that their hot spring waters contained preventative and curative values. By this time, transportation had vastly improved in the American West, particularly in the form of the railroad, allowing people to visit places that would have been inaccessible otherwise. The hot spring resorts at Radium and Montezuma were both products of these developments.

The fashion waned by the outbreak of World War I, and by that time all the major thermal areas of the eastern United States had been developed. In the American West, development of thermal waters was a lot less extensive due to the region's much smaller population density during the same period. Nevertheless, by the 1950s the boom in hot spring resorts had passed, and many closed down or were simply abandoned. Several of these resorts have never reopened, but recently a renewed interest in hot springs has witnessed the reuse of previously abandoned springs, with varying results.

Today there are an estimated 1,800 hot springs in the United States, the majority of which are in the western portion of the country. Out of all the hot springs in America, approximately 115 have been developed into extensive resorts or spas.

Hot Springs in New Mexico

New Mexico, the Land of Enchantment—after visiting the springs in this book, you will be hard-pressed to disagree with this title. New Mexico is also a land of extremes. From the low desert in the south to the pine-clad Rocky Mountains in the north, New Mexico has just about everything in between. The hot springs found in this book also range across the state's geographic diversity. For the most part, however, the springs are concentrated in two main areas, the southwestern part of the state and the north-central portion.

Geothermal activity in those two areas is some of the richest in the country. Many of New Mexico's geothermal resources, unfortunately (or fortunately, depending upon your view), are privately owned, and most of these privately owned hot-water sources are also off-limits to the public. There are, however, enough hot springs, warm springs, and hot wells available for public use to make New Mexico a must-visit for any geothermal enthusiast. The natural beauty of the state, along with the amazing array of outdoor activities, makes visiting the springs doubly rewarding. The hot-water enthusiast will also find that most of New Mexico's hot springs are located in natural settings and remain undeveloped. In some cases, hot springs that were at one time commercially developed have reverted back to a more natural state with the waning popularity of resorts.

Much of the state's history is intricately connected to its hot-water sources. Native New Mexicans used the waters for centuries prior to the arrival of Europeans. Often located along major travel routes, these springs later became well known to Spanish, Mexican, and Anglo pioneers. Hot springs were often the only source of water in a dry landscape, making them that much more valuable. As settlement increased in the state, the springs began to be utilized to a greater extent, and in some cases they were commercialized. Some of the more lavish hot spring resorts in New Mexico were Faywood, Montezuma, and Radium Springs. Today these springs are a shadow of what they were in their heydays, but perhaps you will prefer them in their simpler, rustic states.

THERAPEUTIC ASPECTS

Interestingly, while the therapeutic benefits of hot spring water continue to be touted in several countries, such as Portugal, Japan, Germany, and Czechoslovakia, the fad waned considerably in the United States early in the twentieth century. The practice of balneology is prevalent in Europe and Japan, but largely unknown in America. According to some theories, the decline in the use of hot spring water in medicine in this country is due to establishment of more rigorous medical training and intensive research.

Along with the perceived benefits of hot spring water in medical therapy, many have believed—and continue to believe—in the value of consuming mineral waters. A variety of minerals are claimed to have beneficial values when consumed in certain doses. In the eighteenth century, in fact, this belief served as a motivation for the development of the science of chemistry. Physicians during that period believed in the medical efficacy of certain mineral spring waters, and many pioneers in the field of chemistry got their starts by attempting to reproduce the chemical composition of the water in many of the hot springs. These studies were largely driven by the consumption of carbonated beverages and a desire to know the role gases played in these drinks. Today, following a long period of waning popularity, the bottled water industry is growing at a fast rate. Many of the sources of these bottled waters come from hot spring or mineral spring locations.

GEOLOGY OF HOT SPRINGS

Much is now known about the geological settings of hot springs, the surface manifestations of what geologists term geothermal systems, because many of these systems have been tapped for the generation of electricity, a clean source of energy to replace fossil fuels. Hot springs on the surface of the earth can be no hotter than the boiling point at the earth's surface (100 degrees Celsius, or 212 degrees Fahrenheit). Waters at depth, however, can reach temperatures as high as 400 degrees Celsius, or 752 degrees Fahrenheit! Such super temperatures are possible because the boiling point is raised by the high hydrostatic pressure at great depth and because of the nearness to subsurface molten rock (magma).

The earth's heat originates deep beneath the crust, through the decaying of natural radioactive elements such as uranium, thorium, and potassium. Hot springs generally occur where the earth's heat, in the form of hot or molten rock, exists at relatively shallow depths. Areas of recent or current volcanic activity are obvious locales. Although hot springs are abundant in these regions, the most prevalent—and spectacular—are on the sea floor, far from human view. These underwater springs occur along chains of active submarine volcanoes called spreading centers, places where the earth's plates diverge from one another. Hot springs can also occur in places where there is no obvious source for the heating of the water (far from volcanic areas, for example). These hot springs are either formed from magma bodies at depth with no surface manifestation, or the water itself has come from great depths where there is abundant heat, forced to the surface by some unexplained means.

Hot springs occur because of convection. Just as air above a radiator rises as it expands from being heated, water also rises as it is heated. Rocks are generally full of cracks and fractures, and these inevitably become filled with water as rainwater percolates downward to fill all the voids. This water is collected in porous rocks and kept as groundwater (where well water comes from). In mountainous regions this water sometimes emerges again as springs downhill from where the water first entered the fractured rocks, at times forced to the surface by some impermeable barrier. These

The pools at Wildwood Hot Springs in southwestern New Mexico are filled with natural hot spring water, piped directly from the source across the river. The upper pools are filled first, with the overflow going into the larger lower pool.

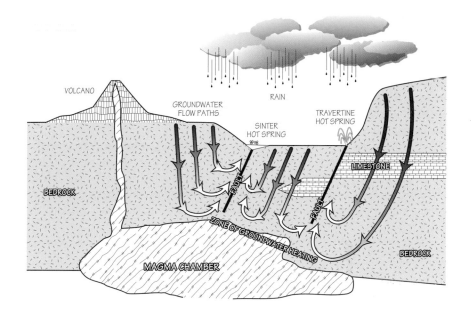

natural cold-water springs occur because of simple gravity flow and differ from hot springs, which flow because of convection.

The convective process that gives rise to hot springs begins with groundwater near a recently injected molten body. The water becomes very hot, even boiling. Such heated water (with associated steam) is less dense than the surrounding cold groundwater, so it rises toward the surface. As it does, cold groundwater instantaneously moves into the void around the magma to replace the rising water, and convection is initiated. The system functions like a coffee percolator. The heated water mixes with overlying water as it rises and loses some of its heat to the rocks through which it passes, eventually discharging at the surface as a hot spring. The pathway of ascent is commonly along a fault because of ease of flow (see diagram). Once such convection systems are set up, they can last for hundreds of years, as heat is slowly harvested from the magma, forcing it to cool and solidify. Water flow, temperature, and the chemical composition of such hot spring waters often remain stable for long periods of time in spite of year-to-year variation in rainfall, suggesting the complex plumbing systems are very deep and large.

The chemical composition of thermal waters is controlled by the rocks through which they pass. For example, some hot springs deposit calcium-carbonate-rich travertine around their orifices, such as Mammoth Hot Springs in Yellowstone National Park. Waters of these springs leach and dissolve calcium carbonate from limestones they traverse in the subsurface. When the thermal waters discharge at the surface, the water effervesces dissolved carbon dioxide (CO_2) gas in the same way soda pop effervesces when the bottle cap is removed. Loss of CO_2 results in the precipitation of calcium carbonate, thus hot springs with travertine are evidence of limestone down below.

In most volcanically active regions where limestone is not present, hot springs deposit siliceous sinter around their orifices, which has an entirely different character than travertine. Sinter is relatively pure silica, the same composition as quartz and the most common constituent of igneous rocks. Silica, which we use for glass, is almost insoluble at room temperature. At the high temperatures at depth in geothermal systems, however, silica is relatively soluble, so the thermal waters leach silica from the rocks. As the waters discharge, the silica becomes supersaturated upon the cooling of the spring, and precipitates as sinter.

These two types of chemical deposits, sinter and travertine, are quite different in character, and tell us much about the subsurface geology through which the hot waters passed.

HOW TO USE THIS BOOK

New Mexico is a diverse state with a substantial number of hot and warm springs scattered throughout. Several of these hot-water sources are actually hot wells, the water discovered accidentally when drilling and diverted for various uses. Many others are truly natural hot springs that can be enjoyed by the general public. Still others consist of warm springs that can also provide nice bathing experiences, especially during the state's hot months, when these springs may be a more attractive alternative to their hotter counterparts. No matter which type you sample, New Mexico's geothermal resources are located in some of the most interesting country you can imagine. Take time to enjoy the state's splendor.

This guide does not pretend to be an exhaustive list of hot springs and hot spring resorts in New Mexico. It is, instead, a guide to and description of some of the best hot springs in the state. Most of the springs you will find in this book are of the natural type. There are a few listings for hot spring resorts, but the focus is on natural hot springs in natural settings. Additionally, this book is not strictly a guide to hot spring soaking. Although many of the springs described offer wonderful bathing experiences, there are several worth visiting simply for other attractions. Many of these springs are in majestic settings, several more are in locations of historical or archaeological interest, and others offer geological interest. Before you visit any of these springs, please read the "Precautions" and "Responsible Behavior" sections.

BOOK ORGANIZATION

This book is organized geographically, to allow for the greatest ease in traveling from one hot spring to the next. Following a short introduction to the spring, all the pertinent information you will need for a visit is provided, such as location, access, best time of year, and nearest services. Detailed directions are given to each spring, followed by a more in-depth discussion and description of the spring itself.

The book is basically divided into two regions: southern New Mexico and northern New Mexico. The lines between the regions were drawn arbitrarily, simply for the sake of organization. In some cases, hot springs in one region may be closer to springs in another region than to those in its own. To find out what other springs are in your vicinity, check the overview map of the state.

The book is further divided into subregions. These subregions were also created arbitrarily, though they are designed to give the reader a sense of place when visiting a hot spring or series of hot springs. Generally, these subregions also follow geographical lines. A short introduction is given for each region and subregion, pointing out some of the more salient features of the country in which readers will find themselves. Historical vignettes are also sometimes included, both to add some flavor to the region and to put the reader far ahead of casual tourists who generally know nothing about the areas they are visiting.

HOW TO FIND THE HOT SPRINGS

Each set of directions is designed to be used in conjunction with the maps provided. These directions have all been field checked and should get you to the spring with minimal confusion. The maps show the important features needed to reach the spring, but the reader needs to pay close attention to mileages stated in the "Finding the spring" portion of the entry. The maps do not always show all the features in the region and are designed to be location aids, not replacements for a topographic map.

It is highly recommended that readers use a standard New Mexico highway map and a US Geological Survey (USGS) topographic map when visiting these springs. A highway map or occasionally a 1:100,000-scale topographic map will generally suffice for most springs that require only a drive to reach them. When hiking is required, however, I strongly recommend obtaining the 1:24,000-scale map. In any case, the recommended map is listed for each spring. Topographic maps can be ordered directly from the USGS (www.usgs.gov). They can also be found at many map stores and some specialty outdoors outlets. It is also recommended that readers obtain a USDA Forest Service map for some of the hot springs located in national forests. In addition, important information such as up-to-date road conditions, access, permit requirements, and weather can usually be obtained from the land management agency with jurisdiction over the hot spring to be visited. Contact information for most of these offices can be found in Appendix B.

New Mexico has many charming and rustic hot springs spas.

PRECAUTIONS

Visiting hot springs carries certain risks and inherent dangers. Hot springs, after all, can contain scalding water. Pay attention to all directions and descriptions given in this book. Most dangers are pointed out to the reader, but not all can be anticipated.

Do not, under any circumstance, get into water without first testing it in some way. You will usually be able to tell how hot a spring is just by approaching the water. If you can feel the heat of the water from a few inches away, it's probably too hot. If the water is steaming, even on a warm day, it also probably is too hot. If the water appears to be fine, put a finger or hand in it to test it. If your hand can't stay submerged without hurting, don't put your body in. More important, if you cannot see the bottom of a spring in any way, don't get in. The water on the top of the spring may be fine, but deeper water may scald you. Also be careful around mud in hot springs, as it can often hide extremely hot water underneath. When in doubt, stay out.

Perhaps one of the most lethal dangers posed by certain hot springs is the presence of the amoeba *Naegleria fowleri*. These amoebas enter human hosts through mucus membranes via the nose, causing an infection resembling meningitis that is nearly always fatal. Just to be safe when visiting these springs, do not put your head under the water or let the water enter your nose or mouth.

If you plan on camping—and even if you don't—make a checklist of equipment needed before heading out. I recommend you bring at least the following:

- ☐ spare tire, jack, lug wrench
- ☐ basic tool kit for the car (screwdrivers, wrenches, hammer, etc.)
- ☐ shelter of some kind (such as a tent)
- ☐ extra clothing (including wet-weather gear)
- ☐ sleeping bag, insulating pad, blankets
- ☐ food and water (more than you will need)
- ☐ stove or other means by which to cook food
- ☐ electrical tape
- ☐ rope
- ☐ shovel
- ☐ ax or small saw
- ☐ firewood
- ☐ candles
- ☐ matches
- ☐ flashlights
- ☐ extra batteries
- ☐ knife
- ☐ first-aid kit

Even if you are planning on only being out for the day, it's not a bad idea to bring along most of this equipment, as you'll be glad you did if you get stranded.

As many of these springs are far from civilization, precautions should be taken. Be sure your vehicle is in sound shape and able to make a long trip. Check all of the engine's fluids, including oil and coolant. Be sure that all the tires have the necessary pressure and that you have a spare (along with a jack and lug wrench). Be sure you know how to change a tire before you head out. By far the most common breakdown is a flat tire, and when driving on dirt roads, you will eventually get a flat. Rocks have a tendency to get caught in your treads, occasionally puncturing the fabric of the tire. Always plan ahead when considering gasoline. Be sure you know how far you are going, your car's gas mileage, and where the next gas station is. The location of the nearest services is given in each of the entries.

Be sure to notify someone of your trip and when you plan on returning. Contact the land management agency for the area to which you are heading to check on access, restrictions, and permit requirements. Be sure to keep a watch on the weather. If storms threaten, stay off secondary dirt roads even if you have four-wheel drive, and off all dirt roads if you have a passenger vehicle. A road may not be wet when you depart but may become impassable during and following a storm. When in the desert portions of the state, be especially aware of thunderstorms and flash floods. Flash floods can occur even when it is not raining where you are. Desert washes can fill with no warning and become raging torrents. Do not under any circumstances make camp in a wash.

As many of the springs in this book require long hikes, be extra prepared when making these trips. Only those in sound physical shape should take the hikes, and some, such as Jordan and Turkey Creek, are recommended for experienced hikers only. Mileages can be deceiving, as many of the routes described do not follow trails or require a fair amount of bushwhacking. Hiking up canyons, for example, will take you more than twice as long as hiking along a trail. This kind of hiking also wears you out faster and is harder on your joints. Letting someone know where you are going and when you are expected back is especially critical for these trips. Do not attempt them alone, and be sure to bring plenty of water and food. The proper maps are also critical for these hiking trips.

RESPONSIBLE BEHAVIOR

Visiting hot springs carries with it a sort of unspoken etiquette. As most of the hot springs described in this book are on public land, you will not be trespassing. A few of the springs are located on private land, and I recommend that you do not trespass. In some cases, the landowner has allowed people to visit the springs on his or her property. In any event, respect private property. If there are "no trespassing" signs, obey them. This will help keep numerous hot springs open to the public—and will prevent you from getting shot.

Some of the springs are located on Indian reservations, and all posted rules should be obeyed. When on public land, also obey all signs. Overnight camping is not permitted at most hot springs, and this is usually posted. Obey these signs, as there are usually campgrounds or other public lands nearby that do not restrict camping.

One of the biggest problems faced by hot spring enthusiasts is vandalism and trash. Most of the well-known hot springs in New Mexico have experienced some aspect of these activities. Graffiti, broken glass, trash, and off-road driving truly detract from the beauty these places hold. Be sure to pack out all trash, stay on established roads, and generally leave things as you found them (or better).

Many of the hot springs described in this book are visited quite often. Do not be surprised to find people already at your hot spring destination. People generally prefer privacy and will appreciate it if you let them finish their soak before you enjoy the water. This is especially true for families and couples. Others may enjoy your company, and a simple inquiry will let you know either way. Many locations offer several soaking opportunities, sometimes quite removed from the other pools.

A lot of people enjoy hot springs without bathing suits. For those springs in remote locations, this is usually the norm. Public bathing facilities or pools in public view typically require clothing, unless you have a private room. You will generally notice the prevalent trend at most springs. Again, obey any and all signs posted and there should be no problem. Nudity has become pervasive at several locations, including Spence, Manby, Black Rock, Faywood, and San Francisco Hot Springs. If nudity offends you, you may not want to visit these places, or you may wish to wait until you can have the springs to yourself. Most of the resorts listed allow visitors to choose for themselves in their private rooms. These locations include the various hot spring resorts in Truth or Consequences, along with Ojo Caliente and Ten Thousand Waves.

AUTHOR'S FAVORITES

HOT SPRINGS CLOSE TO THE CITY
Ten Thousand Waves
If you are in the Santa Fe area, Ten Thousand Waves is well worth a visit. There are few other hot springs this close to New Mexico's larger towns. Ten Thousand Waves, although a little expensive, provides virtually every type of hot-water experience you could ask for. There are numerous private tubs to choose from, along with communal tubs, and a broad array of massages and body treatments. Lodging can also be had on the property.

FOR THE FAMILY
Montezuma Hot Springs
Located immediately off a paved road, Montezuma is easy to reach and is set in a beautiful valley. Families do not need to worry about the nudity crowd at Montezuma, as bathing suits are required. The hot springs are also surrounded by fascinating ruins with an interesting history. Because there are several pools, families should not have too much difficulty finding a bathing spot. Do be careful, however, as some of the pools can be rather hot.

A REMOTE EXPERIENCE
Turkey Creek Hot Springs
If you desire a challenge, both physically and mentally, Turkey Creek Hot Springs is your place. Requiring an 8-mile round-trip hike to visit, Turkey Creek is one of the most remote springs in the book. Although others require more hiking to reach, Turkey Creek is not located along a trail and can be tricky to find. The last few miles of the hike can be difficult, as you thread your way up Turkey Creek Canyon. Once you finally reach the springs, however, you will be richly rewarded. Consisting of numerous seeps of hot and warm water, several bathing opportunities await you. Come prepared!

SOUTHERN NEW MEXICO

A historic gazebo overlooks the pool area at Radium Springs.

SAN FRANCISCO RIVER AREA

A series of hot springs are located along the San Francisco River in western New Mexico. San Francisco Hot Springs and Sundial Springs are located along the lower (southern) portion of the river, prior to where it reenters Arizona. Another hot springs, Frisco Box, lies to the north near the small town of Reserve. San Francisco and Frisco Box require hiking to access, while Sundial includes a campground and hot pools accessible by car.

The group of springs along the lower stretches of the river is known collectively as the San Francisco Hot Springs, though they have been referred to by various names in the past. Because the two accessible springs are located in one general area, I have combined them in one listing. Access to these springs used to be along a forest service road and a short hike along the river. As a result of rampant abuse, and because the route crossed private property, access was blocked. The forest service then opened an alternate route to the south, with a parking area and trailhead. This access route required a longer hike to reach the springs (about 1.5 miles) and resulted in a sharp drop-off in use. The condition of the hot springs and the surrounding area improved as a result, making for a much better visitor experience for those who were willing to make the short hike.

Floods are common in this part of the country, however, and the condition of the access route, the hot springs, and the river itself can change dramatically. This was the case during the summer of 2006. Though most of the access trail remained in place, once at the river all traces of the old trail were obliterated by flooding. The high waters also washed out the baths that had been constructed at the springs. The flow of the springs themselves also appeared to have been altered, though hot water is still flowing. Needless to say, the visitor experience at these hot springs has changed drastically as a result of flooding. Undoubtedly, however, the situation will improve in the future, as the baths are replaced when the water recedes. For more information and the latest access issues, contact the Gila National Forest's Glenwood Ranger Station.

Frisco Box requires a much more vigorous hike than San Francisco Hot Springs, so it receives much less visitation. Unfortunately, access issues have also been a problem at Frisco. The previous route, which had been used for years, was closed by landowners tired of disrespectful visitors. The forest service opened another route that avoided the private property, making it a much longer hike. The trip is well worth it, however, as the surrounding countryside is magnificent. For up-to-date access information, as well as trail conditions and weather, contact the Gila National Forest's Reserve Ranger District.

Be advised that San Francisco, Sundial, and Frisco Box are closer to Turkey Creek Hot Springs than they are to the other listing in this section, Faywood Hot Springs. If you are hoping to combine trips, plan accordingly.

1. SAN FRANCISCO HOT SPRINGS

General description: These two hot springs located along the San Francisco River require a short hike to reach. During high water, baths are generally washed out, though they are rebuilt once the waters recede.

Location: Along the lower San Francisco River in southwestern New Mexico, near the small towns of Glenwood (8 miles) and Pleasanton, and approximately 55 miles northwest of Silver City

Primitive/developed: Primitive. Pools must be constructed with rocks for bathing purposes.

Best time of year: Year-round. During wet weather, the river can be too dangerous to cross and trails may be impossible to locate. This includes times of particularly large spring runoff (February through April), as well as in heavy rains during the monsoon season (July through mid/late September).

Restrictions: The hot springs themselves are on forest service property. There is, however, private property nearby. Several areas are off-limits to vehicle access and camping. Be sure to obey all signs.

Access: The hot springs are accessible via a short drive down a dirt road from the highway and a hike of approximately 1.25 miles. To reach the springs, the river must be crossed several times. The road is generally in good condition and easily passable by most vehicles, although can become impassable when wet.

Water temperature: The springs vary in temperature. The hottest (though inaccessible) are 120 degrees at their source. The lower hot springs are approximately 108 to 110 degrees at their source. Because pools are formed adjacent to the river, their temperatures vary, though generally are about 100 degrees.

Nearby attractions: Sundial Springs; ghost town of Mogollon; Catwalk hike

Services: Only the most basic services are available in Glenwood, approximately 8 miles away. More complete services (gas, food, and lodging) can be found in Silver City, about 55 miles to the southeast.

Camping: Camping is not permitted at the hot springs themselves, but is permitted at the trailhead. Apparently, camping is also permitted downstream of the hot springs approximately a quarter mile. There are also several forest service campgrounds north along US 180.

Map: USGS Dillon Mountain quadrangle (1:24,000 scale)

For more information: Updates on access and restrictions can be obtained from the Gila National Forest, Glenwood Ranger District; (575) 539-2481

Finding the spring: From Silver City, travel north on US 180 for approximately 55 miles. Look for a forest service sign with a hiking symbol (depicting two hikers) just before mile marker 58 and shortly after mile marker 59 (the sign is on the right-hand side of the road, with an arrow pointing to the left). Turn left on this small dirt road (sometimes signed San Francisco Hot Springs), and drive approximately a half mile, past a small campground, to a small parking area with an information board and a toilet. Park here (take all valuables with you), and follow the trail approximately 1.25 miles down to the river. You will pass through a stock fence about 1 mile in, with signs indicating day use, before you begin the descent to the river. This last part of the trail is quite steep and can be slippery with many loose rocks, so be careful.

Once you reach the river, to get to what remains of the middle hot springs (formerly known as Bubbles Hot Springs), cross the river and head for the cliffs on the other bank. Most recently this area was overgrown with vegetation and the trail was hard to see. Look for rock cairns and/or flagging that marks the trail. Eventually you will come to the hot springs on the riverbank. To reach the lower hot springs, instead of crossing the river, find a trail on the left (sometimes with a sign indicating "trail"). Follow the trail downriver for approximately 450 yards to the hot springs on your right. Do not attempt to cross the river during high water—it's dangerous!

Coming from the north, drive approximately 3 miles past Pleasanton, and after crossing the Dugway Bridge, look for the forest service hiking sign. Turn right on the dirt road and follow the directions above.

THE HOT SPRINGS

The San Francisco Hot Springs were a very popular spot for many years. Virtually unregulated access and the increasingly larger number of people visiting them created problems that included trash, parking, crowded pools, and trespassing. As a result, the old access route was blocked, and a new trailhead was established to the south. This access point requires a hike of approximately 1.5 miles, greatly reducing the visitation. The visitor experience is therefore much better, despite the increased hike required. In recent years, numerous floods have altered the landscape considerably. Though the hot springs continue to bubble up from the ground, the routes to access them have changed with the changing nature of the floodplain of the San Francisco River. Thankfully, the hot springs themselves remain, though bathing experiences are not what they used to be.

The two hot springs highlighted here are on forest service land, which officially prohibits nude bathing in this location, and rangers have been known to issue citations. Because of the relative isolation of the hot springs, however, enforcement is rather difficult and lax. Though you may have to share the hot springs with others, the San Francisco River area is beautiful and enjoyable, with much else to see in the vicinity.

This section of the San Francisco River is the most inaccessible portion of this largest tributary to the Gila River. The river itself begins in Arizona (near Alpine), then flows more than 160 miles into New Mexico and eventually back into Arizona. On its route, the river passes through volcanic deposits from the Miocene and Oligocene. The hot springs are located on a beautiful stretch of the river through a narrow canyon. Like many hot springs, the San Francisco Hot Springs are associated with, and likely the result of, a major fault (Sundial Mountain Fault), which bisects the canyon right at the lower hot springs.

Though hot springs bubble up into the river in many places in this area, there are three primary collections of hot springs along this section of the San Francisco River, two of which are accessible.

The San Francisco River is visible from the trail, immediately before you begin your descent to the middle hot springs.

Upper hot springs: These hot springs are surrounded by private property and are not accessible at this time. They are now used for supplying water to nearby Sundial Springs.

Middle hot springs: These hot springs (formerly called "Bubbles") are located immediately across from where the trail first reaches the river, beneath an imposing cliff. Many years ago a large warm pool was in place immediately beneath the cliff, a short distance from the San Francisco River. It was formed by a massive flood that scoured out a portion of the cliff adjacent to the river, uncovering several hot springs. At the same time, the flood deposited a sand bank in front of the hot springs, forming a kind of dam for the water. The pool remained for many years, replenished by the hot spring water bubbling up from the bottom. The large sandy-bottomed pool made for a great bath and was quite popular. Located underneath the cliff, the pool was also almost always shaded.

Subsequent floods altered the shape of the area, and the flow of the hot spring greatly diminished. As a result, there have been no bathing opportunities here for many years. A small warm spring, however, is still in place adjacent to what is left of the large warm pond, which is now an unpleasant, stagnant, and foul-smelling pool. Perhaps someday the bathing opportunities will be reproduced.

Lower hot springs: These springs are located on the same side of the river as the trail, but hiking to them may require crossing the river and back, depending on water level. The springs provide the best potential bathing opportunities in the area.

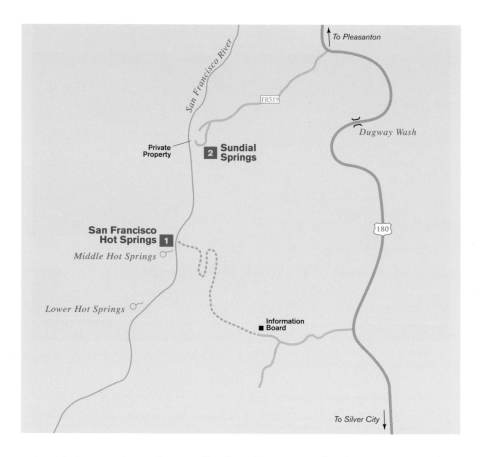

As with the upper hot springs, small rock pools were created in the past, capturing the hot spring water before it entered the river. Recently there were three separate pools, each with slightly different temperatures near 100 degrees. Because they were located immediately adjacent to the river, they frequently filled up with mud. As a result of heavy rains, these lower hot springs were submerged due to summer flooding, and all traces of the rock pools were eliminated. However, the pools were later rebuilt. While it is true that heavy rains can wash the pools out at any time, they are generally rebuilt soon thereafter. It's always best to call the Glenwood Ranger District for the most current information.

For a great place to stay nearby, try Casitas de Gila a short drive away in Gila; www.casitasdegila.com.

2. SUNDIAL SPRINGS

General description: A private campground includes two pools fed by hot spring water pumped to the site.

Location: Along the lower San Francisco River in southwestern New Mexico, south of the small towns of Glenwood and Pleasanton and approximately 60 miles northwest of Silver City

Primitive/developed: Developed

Best time of year: Year-round

Restrictions: This is a private establishment. Reservations are required 48 hours in advance for camping or day use of the tubs. No children are permitted. No RVs over 34 feet in length are allowed.

Access: The small resort is located at the end of a dirt road that is generally passable to all vehicles, except during wet weather.

Water temperature: Pools are maintained at temperatures between 102 and 104 degrees. The temperature of the hot spring source from which these pools are filled is about 120 degrees.

Nearby attractions: San Francisco Hot Springs; ghost town of Mogollon; Catwalk hike

Services: Only the most basic services are available in Glenwood, approximately 5 miles away. More complete services (gas, food, and lodging) can be found in Silver City, about 60 miles to the southeast.

Camping: Tent camping and full RV hookups are available by reservation.

Map: USGS Wilson Mountain quadrangle (1:24,000 scale)

For more information: Sundial Springs; (575) 539-2712; sundialsprings.com

Finding the spring: From Silver City, travel north on US 180 for approximately 60 miles. After mile marker 56, turn left on FR 519. Drive on this generally well-maintained dirt road for 0.5 mile and bear left at a Y. Follow this road for another 0.5 mile to Sundial. The gate will be closed unless you have made prior reservations. From Glenwood, travel south on US 180 for approximately 5 miles (or 2 miles south of Pleasanton) to FR 519. See map on p. 6.

THE HOT SPRINGS

Sundial Springs is a low-key, "niche" establishment consisting of a campground and RV park complete with two pools fed by hot spring water pumped up from the San Francisco River. Set in a beautiful location along the lower San Francisco River, Sundial's campground is perched on a flat with nice views of the surrounding countryside. Wildlife is abundant, and occasionally bighorn sheep are spotted, along with mountain lions, coatimundis, and javelinas.

Sundial is a nice place to camp or simply enjoy the hot pools for the day. The owners require that you call in advance for reservations (575-539-2712). There are currently six RV sites, two tent sites, and one cabin, complete with a queen-size futon and single bed as well as a microwave and small refrigerator. Pools are private, each one rented to one group at a time. Those staying at Sundial are allowed to use the pools for free for one hour. Clothing is optional in the private pools.

The pools vary in size from a maximum of three people in the smallest to ten in the largest, and in price per hour. Remember, reservations are required at least 48 hours in advance, and pools are generally only available Friday through Sunday. Day-use hours are generally 9 a.m. to 5 p.m. During other times, the pools are reserved for the use of those staying in the campground.

3. FRISCO BOX HOT SPRINGS

General description: This small concrete pool of warm water is located along the San Francisco River in the Gila National Forest's San Francisco Mountains. A moderately strenuous hike is required to reach the springs.

Location: Along the upper San Francisco River in western New Mexico, near the small town of Luna

Primitive/developed: Primitive. The small concrete pool does not take away from the beautiful natural setting of the hot springs.

Best time of year: Summer and early fall. Located at 6,500 feet, the access road is closed during most of winter. River levels may be too high during spring runoff.

Restrictions: The hot springs themselves are in the national forest. There is, however, private property adjacent, so be sure to remain on forest service property by following the route to the springs described here.

Access: The hot springs are accessible via a 12-mile drive down a dirt road followed by a moderately strenuous hike of 3.5 miles, with an elevation change of 1,600 feet. The road is usually passable to most vehicles with decent clearance, although it can become impassable when wet.

Water temperature: The spring's source is approximately 98 degrees, cooling in the concrete tub.

Nearby attractions: The Box

Services: Gas, food, and lodging can be found in Alpine, Arizona, approximately 30 miles away. The small town of Reserve, about 25 miles away, has a gas station, store, and two motels. The smaller town of Luna provides a general store.

Camping: Camping is permitted in the national forest surrounding the hot springs; just be sure you are on forest service property. There are several forest service campgrounds in the Gila National Forest; contact the Reserve Ranger District for more information at (575) 533-6231.

Map: USGS Dillon Mountain quadrangle (1:24,000 scale)

For more information: Gila National Forest, Reserve Ranger Station; (575) 533-6231

Finding the spring: From the small town of Luna, take US 180 south for approximately 6.5 miles to FR 35 on your left. From Reserve, travel south on NM 12 to US 180, turn right, and travel 7 miles north. Take FR 35, which is a graded dirt road, for 12 miles to its end at a metal gate. From the gate, backtrack slightly to the saddle of the mountain and look for a small wooden trail sign on the north (you may have to hunt around for a while to find it). You have a 3.5-mile hike ahead of you, with an elevation change of 1,600 feet. The way down is steep, so use care. The trailhead is located at the top of the ridge at what's known as the H Bar V Saddle, and the trail is called the Frisco Divide Trail (#124). Follow the route as it ascends briefly then winds its way along the ridge for less than a mile. Then, the trail descends rapidly to reach the canyon of the San Francisco River. Although there is only one trail, it can be hard to follow at times. The forest service has attempted to improve the trail, and in some places has marked it with flagging or stone markers. Just keep looking for the trail, or signs of the trail.

After 3 miles you will reach the canyon bottom and Frisco Box Trail (#762). Turn right and follow this trail for approximately 0.5 mile. The trail will cross the river twice (sometimes more when the water is high), at which point you should be on the lookout for a smaller trail to the right. Follow this trail for less than 0.25 mile to the small concrete pool on the south bank of the San Francisco River. It is not always easy to find, so keep your eyes open.

The forest service identifies another route to the spring, though it is much longer (7 miles) and takes a great deal more time. From Reserve, go north on NM 12 for 5 miles. Turn left on FR 49 (Toriette Lakes), drive for about 0.25 mile, turn left on FR 41, and drive approximately 5 miles to the trailhead for the Frisco Box Trail (#762). FR 41 crosses several creeks and washes, and is not recommended for passenger vehicles. Follow the Frisco Box Trail for 5.5 miles, where it descends into the canyon of the San Francisco River. At this point, you will follow the gorge of the river for 1.5 miles as it gets more and more narrow, passing through the namesake "Box," where the canyon is at its most narrow. This section may include wading through water as high as your waist or even higher during wet weather. About a mile later, keep an eye out for a smaller trail on the left. Follow it for about 0.25 mile to the warm spring.

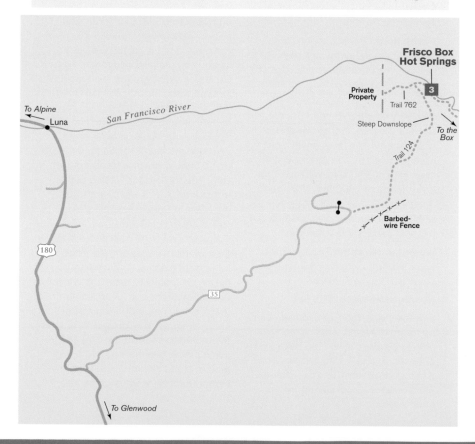

THE HOT SPRINGS

The Frisco Box Hot Springs (also known as Frisco Hot Springs) is actually more of a warm spring, as the 98-degree water cools off considerably in the small concrete tub (about 4 by 8 feet). The tub captures one of several small hot spring seeps along the banks of the San Francisco River. The challenging hike required to reach the spring makes it that much more enjoyable. Unfortunately, you have all the uphill part of the hike on your way out, so be sure to leave plenty of water, food, strength, and sunlight for the return trip. Also, plan that your return will take twice as long as your journey to the springs.

Set in the high pine forest of the San Francisco Mountains, Frisco Box is a great place to visit if you like wilderness solitude. A previous access route required a considerably shorter hike and resulted in much higher visitation at the hot springs. Following problems between visitors to the springs and local landowners, the route was closed. The forest service then opened the route described above, following infrequently used pack trails. The difficulty of the route has decreased visitation considerably.

NEARBY ATTRACTIONS

Mogollon

The ghost town of Mogollon is definitely worth the long drive on a dirt road replete with hairpin turns. Founded in the 1890s, Mogollon quickly rose to prominence due to its silver and gold ore, both of which were mined in abundance. The road you drive on to reach the town was actually constructed in 1897 by convict labor (as were many roads in those days) and, as you will see, had to be hacked out of the hillside in many places.

Twenty-mule teams hauled the ore from the mines in Mogollon to be processed elsewhere. The miners not only had to deal with a difficult access route to and from the mines, but they were also frequently harassed by Apache war parties. Despite the fact that many miners were killed, by 1914 the town supported a nearly $1 million payroll.

Mogollon had declined, like many other mining towns, by 1926, and World War II brought about the end of mining there. The town all but dried up, though a few hardy souls still reside in Mogollon to this day. Please respect this historic area.

From Glenwood, drive 5 miles north on US 180 to a small sign for the road to Mogollon. Turn right (east) here, and follow the unpaved NM 159 for approximately 10 miles to the ghost town. A variety of ruins, buildings, and other structures await you.

The Catwalk

The Catwalk is a wonderful trail route through the narrow canyon of Whitewater Creek. A suspended footbridge (catwalk) has been built along much of this trail, which actually follows the route of a water line built in the 1890s. The scenery is truly incredible. There is also a picnic area, along with the trailhead into the Gila Wilderness. To reach the Catwalk, look for NM 174 immediately north of Glenwood. Turn right and drive approximately 5 miles to the trailhead.

If you have time, be sure to visit the Box, which is where the San Francisco River is constricted into an extremely narrow canyon, just 1 mile farther from the hot springs (continue the same direction along the river). The best way to visit both the Box and the hot springs is to backpack and camp somewhere along the river, as trying to do both in a day trip may be too much. Whatever you do, do not attempt this trip during periods of high water or wet weather.

4. FAYWOOD HOT SPRINGS

General description: This historic hot spring resort has been remodeled over the past several years to provide a rustic atmosphere with a variety of outdoor bathing experiences, as well as camping and other overnight accommodations.

Location: Southwestern New Mexico, equidistant between Silver City to the north and Deming to the south. Located immediately off NM 61, about 2 miles from the intersection of US 180 and NM 61.

Primitive/developed: Developed, though casual in feel. Under almost constant improvement since 1993, Faywood has added numerous enhancements since that time, though it's definitely a rustic experience.

Best time of year: Year-round. Summers can be hot, though still enjoyable (elevation is 5,000 feet).

Restrictions: This is a privately owned resort that is open to the public. All visitors are required to check in at the office to register and pay fees before proceeding to the bathing areas.

Access: The resort is a short drive on a dirt road from a paved highway and is accessible by any vehicle.

Water temperature: The source is an amazingly constant 137 degrees. The pools vary in temperature, ranging from about 95 to 110 degrees. The private tubs' temperatures can be regulated by the user.

Nearby attractions: City of Rocks State Park; Gila Wilderness; Silver City

Services: Lodging is available at Faywood in the form of several one-bedroom cabins. Gas and food are available in Hurly, 12 miles away. Gas, food, and lodging can be found in Deming, approximately 26 miles to the south.

Camping: Several camping options are available at Faywood: tent sites, RV spaces, as well as cabins.

Maps: New Mexico state highway map; USGS Hatch quadrangle (1:100,000 scale)

For more information: Contact Faywood Hot Springs; (575) 536-9663; faywoodsprings@gmail.com

Finding the spring: From Deming, head northwest out of town on US 180 for approximately 24 miles to a sign for the City of Rocks State Park. Turn right on NM 61 here, and drive approximately 2 miles to the sign for Faywood on the left. Turn onto the small dirt road, and follow it to the parking area and office. From Silver City, proceed south on US 180 for approximately 15 miles to the small town of Hurly, and continue another 10 miles to NM 61 on the left.

THE HOT SPRINGS

Faywood is a unique, historic hot spring resort offering a variety of outdoor bathing experiences in a relaxed, casual setting. The natural hot water flows out of the top of a large travertine hill at 137 degrees. From there the water is diverted into several pool areas, where it cools off to more comfortable temperatures for bathing (95 to 110 degrees). The pool areas are all outside, though shaded by large sail-cloth coverings. There are both clothing-required and clothing-optional public bathing areas, separated by privacy fencing, and each contains several pools to choose from. Five private

There are several pools to choose from in the clothing-optional section at Faywood Hot Springs.

tubs are also available for rent by the hour. Both clothing-required and clothing-optional campgrounds are also available, as well as a variety of cabins to choose from for overnight stays.

The grounds around the pool areas are well vegetated, with footpaths throughout, providing a peaceful and tranquil atmosphere. Dressing rooms and pit toilets are located nearby, and towels and bathing suits can be rented at the office. There are also massage therapy services available on-site. A large visitor center is currently under construction and will eventually house a museum, gift shop, and cafe. A large swimming pool is also being built, as is an entirely new entrance.

Faywood is a very popular spot and can be particularly busy on holiday weekends, though drop-in visitors are always welcome. Day use does not require a reservation, though reservations for overnight accommodations are recommended. The gates are open from 10 a.m. to 10 p.m. seven days a week. Prices are based on a day rate for the public pools and by the hour for the private pools. Public pools are free to overnight guests and open to them all night. Group discounts for parties of ten or more are available. Contact Faywood for current prices.

The hot springs at Faywood were well utilized by Native Americans for centuries, as mortar holes (for grinding seeds and other foodstuffs) attest. Evidence suggests that the ancient Mimbres culture used the springs, as well as the more recent Apache. The springs are mentioned in many early Euro-American accounts of travel through the area. This is not surprising, as the springs are located along what was a relatively major travel corridor between present-day New Mexico and Arizona. The springs were first commercially used in 1876, when Colonel Richard Hudson constructed the Hudson Hotel there. Many people journeyed to the springs for enjoyment as well as to cure a variety of ailments. Unfortunately, the hotel burned down in 1892, but in 1894 another hotel was built, this one much larger than the previous. Andrew Graham's Casa de Consuelo (House of Comfort) contained sixty rooms. Its luxuriance attested to the popularity of hot springs in the late nineteenth century, and the belief in mineral water's curative abilities.

At roughly the turn of the twentieth century, three men—T. C. McDermott, J. C. Fay, and W. Lockwood—purchased the resort, and the name Faywood was first used (combining Fay and Lockwood). Throughout the next few decades, Faywood enjoyed a popularity not found at most other hot spring resorts of the time. Many people from Silver City and Deming made regular trips to the springs. Like other such resorts, however, Faywood also declined in popularity, and by 1951 the buildings were destroyed. The property passed through many hands until Kennecott Copper acquired it in 1966 (allowing people to continue using the hot springs on a casual basis), followed by the Phelps Dodge Company. By this time, in the 1980s, the property was fenced and closed to the public. The land was sold in 1993 to Wanda G. Fuselier and Elon M. Yurwitand, who set about developing a rustic hot springs resort. Subsequent owners, as well as the Shirks, current owners since 2011, have also been making improvements and enhancements to it ever since.

GILA HOT SPRINGS AND THE GILA WILDERNESS AREA

Designated the nation's first wilderness area in 1924, the Gila Wilderness has not changed much since. If you enjoy unspoiled wilderness, far from civilization and relatively free of people, this is the place for you. The Gila Wilderness area is surrounded by the Gila National Forest, which contains everything from low desert scrub to high pine forests. This is the headwaters of the mighty Gila River, which flows across the entire state of Arizona, eventually reaching the Colorado River at the California/Arizona state line.

The Gila Wilderness is a haven for hot springs. The Gila Mountains are volcanic in origin, having only recently (in geologic time) been formed. The volcanic activity in the area explains the plethora of hot springs in a relatively small geographic area. The hot springs themselves occur along a somewhat regular north–south trend, formed by hot water at depth forced to the surface along a few fault lines in what is termed a graben. Hot water (approximately 165 degrees at the source) from the Gila Hot Springs is not only used for several baths, but also for home heating. Many hot springs, both developed (Wildwood, Wilderness Lodge, Gila Hot Springs RV Park and Campground) and primitive (Melanie, Jordan, Middle Fork, Meadows), can be enjoyed while in the area.

There are ample recreational opportunities in the Gila Wilderness. Hiking, backpacking, fishing, and horseback riding are just some of the more common ones. The wildlife is also rich, particularly in birds. The archaeological wealth of the area is capped by the Gila Cliff Dwellings National Monument, at the end of NM 15. People have lived in the area of the Gila Cliff Dwellings for the past 12,000 years. Several Native American cultures occupied the area, most of whom lived there only seasonally. The Mogollon culture, however, arriving in the late 1200s, built and lived in what are now preserved rock dwellings in the cliff's caves. They appear to have remained through the 1300s and were followed by subsequent cultures, including the Apache.

A small army camp was established in the late 1800s at what is now Gila Hot Springs to protect settlers from the Apaches. The area appears to have been first settled by whites in the 1880s, by the Hill brothers, with the first houses built sometime around 1890. In 1929 Doc Campbell came to the area to ranch cattle, and in 1940 he acquired much of the property encompassing the Gila Hot Springs. Hot spring water supplied his ranch as well as a natural spa, which he opened to the public. In 1963 he built Doc Campbell's Post, now known as Doc Campbell's Post and Vacation Center.

At the turn of the twentieth century another hot spring resort was built along the East Fork of the Gila River by a wealthy cattle rancher, Thomas Lyons. Lyons's elaborate lodge hosted many famous people seeking the solitude of the Gila Wilderness. Building materials and furnishings for this grand lodge were brought to the area by mule train, taking several days from Silver City.

Visitors had to follow treacherous trails and, for a time, a difficult dirt road to reach Gila Hot Springs until an improved automobile road was finally built in 1966.

There are several wonderful bathing pools to choose from at Gila Hot Springs.

The difficulty in reaching the area maintained its isolation for years. The road to Gila Hot Springs and the Gila Wilderness, now NM 15, is still narrow and marked with countless hairpin turns. Allow plenty of time (about two hours) to make the nearly 40-mile drive from Silver City.

The town of Gila Hot Springs is today a small community located near the end of NM 15, 4 miles east of the Gila Cliff Dwellings National Monument (where NM 15 ends). You can still visit Doc Campbell's Post and Vacation Center, which has stayed in the Campbell family, where you can stock up with supplies and get information on the surrounding countryside. The Gila Hot Springs Ranch (also in the Campbell family) operates the Gila Hot Springs RV Park and Campground, which offers lodging in several fully furnished units in addition to the RV park and campground.

For the latest access information on backcountry hot springs, as well as trail conditions and weather, visit the Gila Visitor Center at the end of NM 15, or contact the Gila National Forest's Wilderness Ranger District; www.fs.usda.gov/gila; (575) 536-2250.

5. MELANIE HOT SPRINGS

General description: This fantastic set of natural hot springs is along a remote portion of the upper Gila River. Bathing opportunities include three little rock pools and a small warm waterfall. A short hike of 1.5 miles along and through the Gila River is required.

Location: Southwestern New Mexico, near the small community of Gila Hot Springs

Primitive/developed: Primitive. There has been no development short of the creation of small soaking pools, which frequently have to be rebuilt.

Best time of year: Summer and early fall. Because of the number of crossings of the Gila River, access to the site should not be attempted during high spring runoff or following periods of extensive rainfall (winter and summer monsoons).

Restrictions: The hot springs are located in the Gila National Forest in a designated wilderness area. This basically means no motorized vehicles, which would be impossible in this rugged area anyway.

Access: Melanie Hot Springs can be reached only by foot or horseback, down an approximately 1.5-mile trail that crosses the Gila River eight times.

Water temperature: The source is about 111 degrees. The water cools off to approximately 90 degrees in the small pools and warm waterfall.

Nearby attractions: Gila Hot Springs; Middle Fork Hot Springs; Gila Cliff Dwellings National Monument

Services: There are no services at the hot springs themselves. The most basic necessities (gas and some groceries) can be found at Doc Campbell's, approximately 2 miles to the north. Lodging and showers are also available through the Gila Hot Springs Ranch. More complete services are two hours (40 miles) away in Silver City.

Camping: Grapevine Campground is located at the trailhead. There are also forest service campgrounds near the Gila Cliff Dwellings National Monument and a small campground at Gila Hot Springs with pit toilets and water. Private campgrounds nearby include Wildwood Hot Springs and Gila Hot Springs RV Park.

Map: USGS Gila Hot Springs quadrangle (1:24,000 scale)

For more information: Gila National Forest, Wilderness Ranger District; (575) 536-2250; or the Gila Visitor Center in the national monument; www.nps.gov/gicl/planyourvisit/visitor centers.htm; (575) 536-9461

Finding the spring: From Silver City, travel north on NM 15 to Pinos Altos. Continue north on NM 15 through Pinos Altos for approximately 37.5 miles, into the Gila Wilderness area, to the Grapevine Campground on the right, immediately before a bridge crossing the Gila River. Turn right onto the dirt road (East Fork Road, but it may not be labeled as such). Alternatively, from Gila Hot Springs, travel south on NM 15 for 2 miles to the campground immediately after crossing the bridge and turn left on the dirt road. As you drive down the dirt road, stay to the left for the trailhead parking area (the campground is to the right). Park here, and get ready to hike for 1.5 miles downstream. Follow a faint trail leading under the highway bridge and immediately crossing the river. This is Trail #724, known as the Gila River Trail. The trail crosses the river eight times before reaching the hot springs and can be hard to spot at times. You may wind up crossing the river more or less than eight times if you venture off the trail, but as long as the river is not too high, it doesn't matter too much. Keep an eye on the left (east) bank of the river for the extra-heavy foliage that indicates where the hot springs emanate. You will know that you have gone too far if you get to a large horseshoe-shaped bend in the river. The hot springs are upstream approximately 100 yards from this bend.

Melanie Hot Springs can also be accessed from the Alum Camp Trail (Trail #788). The trailhead for this route is located approximately 1 mile south of the Grapevine Campground on NM 15, on the right side when traveling south. This route is rugged and steep, dropping 1,500 feet to the Gila River in 1.5 miles. Once at the river, turn right and hike about 1 mile up it, crossing the river three times before reaching the hot springs. This route is much more difficult than the main access route described above.

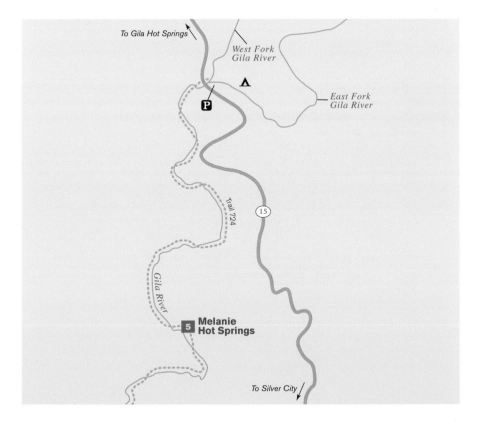

THE HOT SPRINGS

Melanie Hot Springs consist of two small seeps in a steep hillside overlooking the Gila River. The sources are obscured by vegetation, but they flow into three small pools. The first pool is actually a little grotto, with only about 2 feet of warm water. The other two pools are at the base of the cliff and were created by volunteers with rocks and sand. The hot springs also form a small warm waterfall between the grotto and the pools. Sometimes the water eventually flows into the Gila River, where people often build little pools to mix the warm water with the cold river water. Don't count on this, however, for helping you find the hot springs, as there is often either insufficient water to flow all the way to the river, or these pools have been washed out by high water.

Do not attempt this trip when water levels are high in the Gila River, generally during spring runoff or following summer monsoon rains. The river can be fast-moving and hazardous during these periods. The trailhead for Melanie Hot Springs is located immediately below the confluence of the East and West Forks of the Gila River, and hence flow is greatly enhanced downstream.

6. GILA HOT SPRINGS

General description: A collection of high-temperature hot springs along the West Fork of the Gila River supplies several pools in an undeveloped campground and day-use area.

Location: Southwestern New Mexico, in the small community of Gila Hot Springs

Primitive/developed: Developed, though only with the creation of the pools and an unimproved campground.

Best time of year: Year-round. Because Gila Hot Springs are located at a high altitude, road conditions can be difficult in winter.

Restrictions: The springs are located on private property. The pools in the campground can be used by campers or by day users. All campground regulations must be obeyed.

Access: The hot springs are located a short distance off NM 15 on a dirt road. Most cars should have no trouble reaching the springs, but the road can be difficult when wet.

Water temperature: The source is approximately 150 degrees, though the water cools off to between 108 and 110 degrees in the pools.

Nearby attractions: Melanie Hot Springs; Middle Fork Hot Springs; Gila Cliff Dwellings National Monument

Services: The most basic necessities (gas and some groceries) can be found at Doc Campbell's, less than 1 mile away. Lodging and showers are also available through the Gila Hot Springs Ranch. More complete services are two hours (40 miles) away in Silver City.

Camping: There is a small, undeveloped campground at Gila Hot Springs with pit toilets and water. The campground is primarily for tents, though can accommodate RVs under 24 feet in length (no hookups). Gila Springs RV Park and Campground is across NM 15, complete with showers and hot tub. Several forest service campgrounds are located near the Gila Cliff Dwellings National Monument.

Map: USGS Gila Hot Springs quadrangle (1:24,000 scale)

For more information: Contact Gila Hot Springs Ranch; (575) 536-9944; gilahotspringscampground.com

Finding the spring: From Silver City, travel north out of town on NM 15 to Pinos Altos. Continue north on NM 15 through Pinos Altos for approximately 38 miles into the Gila Wilderness area. Immediately before reaching the small community of Gila Hot Springs, turn right on Access Road, with signs for the Wildwood and the Gila River campgrounds. Take Access Road past Jackass Road and follow it downhill for approximately 0.2 mile, then turn left on West Fork Road, paralleling the river. The campground and hot springs will be on your right. Register and pay fees at the self-service board.

THE HOT SPRINGS

First developed in 1992 by Allen and Carla Campbell, Gila Hot Springs Campground has a very rustic, easy-going feel. Allen is the son of Doc and Ida Campbell, who developed many of the visitor services in this remote area. Water from Gila Hot Springs is piped across the West Fork of the Gila River to several pools in a campground and day-use area. The pool closest to the pipe is almost scalding in temperature,

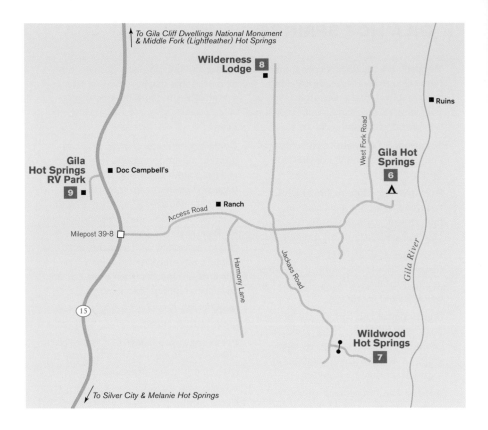

To Gila Cliff Dwellings National Monument & Middle Fork (Lightfeather) Hot Springs

Wilderness Lodge **8**

■ Ruins

West Fork Road

Gila Hot Springs RV Park **9** ■

■ Doc Campbell's

Gila Hot Springs **6**

■ Ranch

Access Road

Milepost 39-8 ☐

15

Harmony Lane

Jackass Road

Gila River

Wildwood Hot Springs **7**

To Silver City & Melanie Hot Springs

while the others are deeper and cooler (between 108 and 110 degrees). The pools are lined with rocks and have sandy bottoms, and there are several to choose from, some large enough for an entire family and others more intimate. The grounds have been improved with a variety of landscaping and art. Bathing suits are required during the day, while after dark clothing may be optional at the discretion of all users in the pools.

The setting is fantastic, located on the banks of the rushing Gila River. You can see the Gila Hot Springs themselves from the campground if you look upstream. Several ruins and foundations are present, along with the unusual colored rock and travertine. Keep in mind that the campground is on, and is surrounded by, private property. A fee is charged for camping per person per night (with full use of the hot pools); a day use per person is also charged. Pit toilets and water are available. Reservations are recommended for camping. As registration is self-service, cash is required (no credit cards accepted).

7. WILDWOOD RETREAT AND HOT SPRINGS

General description: A casual, rustic hot spring resort on the banks of the Gila River offers hot pools, camping and other overnight accommodations, and group-use facilities.

Location: Southwestern New Mexico, near the small community of Gila Hot Springs

Primitive/developed: Developed, though casual in feel

Best time of year: Late spring, summer, and early fall. Wildwood is closed in winter.

Restrictions: Wildwood is a privately owned resort open to day use as well as camping and other overnight accommodations.

Access: The hot springs are located a short distance off NM 15 on a dirt road that is generally passable to all vehicles, but can become muddy during wet weather.

Water temperature: The source is approximately 150 degrees, with temperatures in the baths ranging from 103 to 105 degrees in the two smaller pools and cooler in the larger pool.

Nearby attractions: Melanie Hot Springs; Middle Fork Hot Springs; Gila Hot Springs; Gila Cliff Dwellings National Monument

Services: In addition to campsites, there are a few new overnight accommodations consisting of a straw bale hogan and small cabin. A communal kitchen, modern restrooms, and showers are also available to guests. Gas and some groceries can be found at Doc Campbell's, less than 1 mile away. Lodging and showers are also available through the Gila Hot Springs Ranch. More complete services are two hours (40 miles) away in Silver City.

Camping: There are 25 campsites at Wildwood, both car-camping and walk-in. The undeveloped walk-in sites are located immediately next to the Gila River, near the pools. There is also a small campground nearby at Gila Hot Springs with pit toilets and water. Gila Hot Springs RV Park also has a campground, and several forest service campgrounds are located near the Gila Cliff Dwellings National Monument.

Map: USGS Gila Hot Springs quadrangle (1:24,000 scale)

For more information: Contact Wildwood Retreat and Hot Springs; (575) 536-3600; wildwoodhotspringsretreat.com

Finding the spring: From Silver City, travel north out of town on NM 15 to Pinos Altos. Continue on NM 15 through Pinos Altos for approximately 38 miles into the Gila Wilderness area. Immediately prior to reaching the small community of Gila Hot Springs, turn right on Access Road, with signs for the Wildwood and the Gila River campgrounds. Follow this dirt road downhill for approximately 0.25 mile. Turn right on Jackass Road, with a sign to Wildwood. Follow this small road for less than 0.5 mile to Wildwood on the left. See map on p. 22.

THE HOT SPRINGS

Wildwood Hot Springs was recently reopened with several changes from previous years. The facility is designed to be a retreat, with riverside camping as well as a small collection of overnight accommodations, in a relaxed atmosphere. Hot spring water

A stage is available for special events at Wildwood's group area.

is piped upstream from Gila Hot Springs into several tubs and pools. The water first emerges into two smaller pools (8 by 5 by 2 feet), which are the hottest (between 103 and 105 degrees). The water then overflows into a larger pool (20 by 20 by 3 feet), where it cools off substantially (varying in temperature depending upon the weather). The pools are surrounded by a patio area, which is enclosed by privacy fencing and shaded by numerous large trees. Bathing suits are required during daylight hours, whereas clothing is optional after sunset. Reservations are recommended, but drop-in visitors are always welcome. The retreat is closed in winter.

A campers' lounge complete with kitchen (refrigerator, oven, microwave, and coffee pots), propane stoves, and barbeques is available to guests, along with modern bathroom and shower facilities. Wildwood also has a group area with a full kitchen available for a variety of special events (weddings, meetings, get-togethers, reunions, etc.), along with a fish pond area and zen garden. Towel and bathing suit rentals are available. A per-person fee is charged for day use (10 a.m. to 6 p.m.), and includes use of pools and showers. A per-person camping fee is charged per night, as is a rental fee for the cabins, and for the group area. Special group retreat rental rates are also available for the entire facility.

8. THE WILDERNESS LODGE

General description: This historic lodge and hot spring formerly offered individual rooms for rent, but now the entire facility must be rented at once.

Location: Southwestern New Mexico, in the small community of Gila Hot Springs

Primitive/developed: Developed, though definitely a rustic and casual atmosphere. There is no cell reception, Wi-Fi, or TV.

Best time of year: The lodge is open year-round, though spring, summer, and fall tend to be the better months to visit, as winters can be cold and wet.

Restrictions: This is a privately owned lodge, and must be rented out in its entirety. Reservations are highly recommended. The hot pools are for those renting the entire facility only.

Access: The lodge is located a short distance off NM 15 on a dirt road. Generally, this road is passable to all vehicles, but can become muddy during wet weather.

Water temperature: The source is approximately 150 degrees, cooling off in the pools to between 98 degrees and the low 100s.

Nearby attractions: Wildwood Hot Springs; Melanie Hot Springs; Middle Fork Hot Springs; Gila Hot Springs; Gila Cliff Dwellings National Monument

Services: The Wilderness Lodge offers overnight accommodations with complimentary breakfast. The lodge can sleep sixteen, with single rooms upstairs with shared bathrooms, and a two-bedroom suite with a private bath downstairs. Gas and some groceries can be found at Doc Campbell's, less than 1 mile away. More complete services are two hours (40 miles) away in Silver City.

Camping: There is no camping at the lodge, but there are many options close by, including Wildwood Hot Springs, Gila Hot Springs, Gila Hot Springs RV Park, and several forest service campgrounds near the Gila Cliff Dwellings National Monument.

Map: USGS Gila Hot Springs quadrangle (1:24,000 scale)

For more information: Contact the Wilderness Lodge; (575) 536-9749; www.gilahot.com/index.shtml; wildernesslodge@gilahot.com

Finding the spring: From Silver City, travel north out of town on NM 15 to Pinos Altos. Continue on NM 15 through Pinos Altos for approximately 38 miles into the Gila Wilderness area. Immediately prior to reaching the small community of Gila Hot Springs, turn right on Access Road, with signs for the Wildwood and Gila River campgrounds. Follow this dirt road downhill for approximately 0.25 mile. Turn left on Jackass Road, and the Wilderness Lodge is a short distance ahead on the left. See map on p. 22.

THE HOT SPRINGS

Two hot spring pools are located on the property of the Wilderness Lodge. The rock-lined, gravel-bottomed pools are several feet deep and wide, and are situated close to the lodge behind a small adobe privacy wall. The Wilderness Lodge consists of a large historic building that was originally a schoolhouse in Hurley before it was

There are two pools to choose from immediately adjacent to the Wilderness Lodge building.

moved to Gila Hot Springs in the 1960s. Today it is a rustic retreat offering very simple accommodations and hot spring pools. The lodge has five bedrooms upstairs with two shared bathrooms and a two-bedroom suite downstairs with its own bathroom. Guests receive a complimentary breakfast and use of the pools. Contact the resort for more information on the full-facility rental fee or for reservations.

9. GILA HOT SPRINGS RV PARK AND CAMPGROUND

General description: A small RV park and campground is located in the town of Gila Hot Springs, complete with showers and hot-spring-fed Jacuzzi bath.

Location: Southwestern New Mexico, in the small community of Gila Hot Springs

Primitive/developed: Developed. The hot springs are piped into the park's Jacuzzi.

Best time of year: Year-round, though winters can be cold and wet.

Restrictions: This is a privately owned RV park and campground. Reservations are recommended. The Jacuzzi is available for day use.

Access: Gila Springs RV Park and Campground is located immediately off NM 15.

Water temperature: The source of the hot spring is approximately 120 degrees, though the temperature in the Jacuzzi is cooler.

Nearby attractions: Melanie Hot Springs; Gila Hot Springs; Middle Fork Hot Springs; Wildwood Hot Springs; Gila Cliff Dwellings National Monument

Services: A few furnished apartments are available at the RV park. Gas and food can be found at Doc Campbell's, across NM 15. More complete services are available in Silver City (40 miles away).

Camping: RV hookups and tent camping are available. There are also many other options close by, including Wildwood Hot Springs, Gila Hot Springs, and several forest service campgrounds near the Gila Cliff Dwellings National Monument.

Map: USGS Gila Hot Springs quadrangle (1:24,000 scale)

For more information: Contact Gila Hot Springs Ranch; (575) 536-9314; http://gilahotsprings.com/index.htm; gilahotspringsranch@gilanet.com

Finding the spring: From Silver City, travel north out of town on Highway 15 to Pinos Altos. Continue on Highway 15 through Pinos Altos for approximately 39 miles to the small community of Gila Hot Springs. The RV park and campground will be on your left, across the highway from Doc Campbell's. See map on p. 22.

THE HOT SPRINGS

A part of the Gila Hot Springs Ranch, the park offers fully furnished apartment rooms, several RV hookups, and tent camping in a peaceful setting among numerous cottonwood trees. It is located across the highway from Doc Campbell's store, and is centrally located for adventures in the wilderness area. The park also offers a Jacuzzi fed by the Gila Hot Springs (on the other side of the Gila River), as well as showers. Fees are charged for RV hookups per night, weekly, and monthly. A per-person fee is charged for tent camping. The Jacuzzi is free for campers; a per-person fee is charged otherwise.

10. MIDDLE FORK (LIGHTFEATHER) HOT SPRINGS

General description: A wonderful set of hot springs along the Middle Fork of the Gila River requires a short hike to reach. Although occasionally washed out by floods, small pools for bathing can usually be found.

Location: Southwestern New Mexico, near the small community of Gila Hot Springs

Primitive/developed: Primitive. The hot springs are located in a wilderness area, requiring a short hike to reach them. The only development consists of the creation of rock-lined bathing pools, which are occasionally washed out by flooding.

Best time of year: Summer and early fall. Access to the springs should not be attempted during high spring runoff or following periods of extensive rainfall (winter and summer monsoons).

Restrictions: The springs are within the Gila Wilderness, which means motorized vehicles are not allowed. Otherwise, there are no restrictions.

Access: The hot springs are along the Middle Fork of the Gila River and require a hike of approximately 0.5 mile, including crossing the river at least twice (possibly more during high water).

Water temperature: The source is approximately 149 degrees, but the water cools off as it mixes with the river water in the rock-lined pools. The temperature in the pools, of course, will vary depending upon the mixture of hot and cold water.

Nearby attractions: Melanie Hot Springs; Gila Hot Springs; Gila Cliff Dwellings National Monument

Services: There are no services at the hot springs themselves. The most basic necessities (gas and some groceries) can be found at Doc Campbell's, approximately 2 miles from the trailhead. Lodging and showers are available through the Gila Hot Springs Ranch. More complete services are two hours (40 miles) away in Silver City.

Camping: There are several forest service campgrounds near the Gila Cliff Dwellings National Monument and a small campground at Gila Hot Springs, with pit toilets and water. Private campgrounds nearby include Wildwood Hot Springs and Gila Hot Springs RV Park.

Map: USGS Gila Hot Springs quadrangle (1:24,000 scale)

For more information: Gila National Forest, Wilderness Ranger Station; or the Gila Visitor Center in the national monument; www.nps.gov/gicl/plan yourvisit/visitorcenters.htm; (575) 536-9461

Finding the spring: From Silver City, travel north out of town on NM 15 to Pinos Altos. Continue on NM 15 through Pinos Altos for approximately 39 miles to the small community of Gila Hot Springs. Continue through town, following signs for the Gila Cliff Dwellings National Monument. Stay on NM 15 for 2 miles and turn right to the visitor center (going straight takes you to the cliff dwellings themselves), where you should stop for up-to-date information on river levels and access issues. Continue through the parking lot and turn right on a road at the end of the lot. Drive up a hill and turn left into the trailhead's small dirt parking area. Park here and follow the Middle Fork Trail (#157), which begins at the end of the parking area.

The Middle Fork Trail will lead you down to the Middle Fork of the Gila River, which you will soon cross. Continue another 0.25 mile on the other side of the river, where the trail crosses the river again. From the second crossing, continue less than 0.25 mile upstream, keeping an eye out on the right (east) bank of the river. Slightly upstream of a small rock overhang, you will see the small hot spring source flowing into the river. There may or may not be rock-lined pools along the river, depending upon the time of year you are there.

THE HOT SPRINGS

Middle Fork (sometimes referred to as Lightfeather) is a wonderful hot spring to visit, requiring a short hike. The springs are well known, but the most casual hot spring enthusiasts will be put off by the hike required. Be prepared to get wet (generally up to your knees) during the 0.5-mile hike. There is no way to avoid crossing the river twice.

The springs themselves are very hot (approximately 149 degrees), and will scald you if you sample them near the source. The only way to enjoy the hot water is in one of the rather ephemeral rock-lined pools along the river. The hot spring water mixes with the cold river water, making for a comfortable bath. During high river levels, however, the pools will be washed out and leave you with no bathing options. Try to

The source for Middle Fork Hot Springs bubbles out of the ground at the base of the hill adjacent to the Middle Fork of the Gila River.

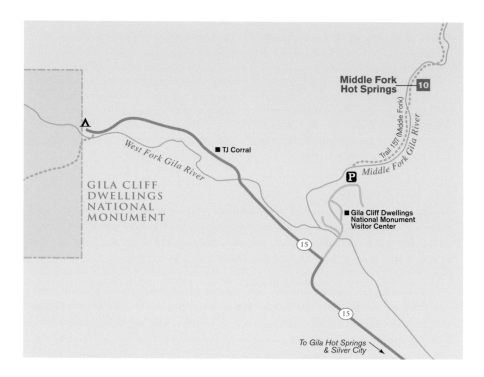

visit the springs during the late summer or early fall. Middle Fork Hot Springs tend to be visited rather heavily, as they are located on a well-traveled trail into the Gila Wilderness backcountry. Don't be surprised by the presence of other hikers, or those on horseback.

Legend holds that the famed Apache leader Geronimo may have been born at these hot springs, though more modern scholarship places his birthplace closer to Clifton, Arizona. The Apache presence in these mountains is unmistakable, however, as indicated by Spanish journals as well as more recent Anglo accounts. The hot springs were utilized by the Apaches, who built a small structure over the Middle Fork Hot Springs to use for bathing. Thankfully, the area has changed little since that time.

11. JORDAN HOT SPRINGS

General description: This remote hot spring in the Gila Wilderness of the Mogollon Mountains requires a moderately difficult hike to reach, and is recommended as a backpack trip over two days, though the hike can be done in one long day.

Location: Southwestern New Mexico in the remote Gila Wilderness, near the town of Gila Hot Springs

Primitive/developed: Primitive. There has been no development of this hot spring except for the creation of bathing pools.

Best time of year: Summer and early fall. The hot springs are located high in the Mogollon Mountains, along the Middle Fork of the Gila River, and are only accessible when there are low water levels on the river. Do not attempt the trip during periods of high water.

Restrictions: The springs are within the Gila Wilderness, which means motorized vehicles are not allowed. Otherwise, there are no restrictions.

Access: A 6.5-mile hike (one way) is required to reach the hot springs. The last 2 miles of this route require walking in and out of the Middle Fork of the Gila River.

Water temperature: The source is approximately 94 degrees, making it more of a warm spring. The temperature does make for an excellent bathing experience, however.

Nearby attractions: The Meadows Warm Springs; Gila Hot Springs; Middle Fork Hot Springs; Gila Cliff Dwellings National Monument

Services: There are no services at the hot springs themselves. The most basic necessities (gas and some groceries) can be found at Doc Campbell's, approximately 2 miles from the trailhead. Lodging and showers are also available at the Gila Hot Springs Ranch. More complete services are two hours (40 miles) away in Silver City.

Camping: Undeveloped camping is permitted within the wilderness area, and there are many good places to camp along the way. There are several forest service campgrounds near the Gila Cliff Dwellings National Monument and a small campground at Gila Hot Springs with pit toilets and water. Private campgrounds nearby include Wildwood Hot Springs and Gila Hot Springs RV Park.

Maps: USGS Gila Hot Springs and Woodland Park quadrangles (1:24,000 scale)

For more information: Gila National Forest, Wilderness Ranger District; www.fs.usda.gov/gila; (575) 536-2250; or the Gila Visitor Center in the national monument; www.nps.gov/gicl/planyourvisit/visitorcenters.htm; (575) 536-9461

Finding the spring: From Silver City, travel north out of town on NM 15 to Pinos Altos. Continue on NM 15 through Pinos Altos for approximately 39 miles toward the Gila Wilderness. Drive through the small town of Gila Hot Springs, following signs for the Gila Cliff Dwellings National Monument, and stay on NM 15 for 2 miles. Stop at the visitor center for up-to-date information on river levels and access issues, then go back toward the Gila Cliff Dwellings. About 1 mile from the intersection with the road to the visitor center, you will see a parking area for TJ Corral. Turn right here, and park at the trailhead.

Take Trail #729 (Bear Canyon Trail) north (uphill). At 0.25 mile in, turn right and stay on Trail #729. You will climb almost 1,000 feet on this trail for the first 2 miles before reaching the summit at the intersection with Trail #164 (Meadows Trail) on your left. Continue straight on Trail #729, which will then descend into the narrow drainage of Little Bear Canyon. The trail will then intersect Trail #157 (Middle Fork Trail), which you will take to the left (you are now 4.5 miles from TJ Corral).

Trail #157 follows the river, and several crossings will be required from here on. Hike for about 2 miles upstream, crossing the river 15 times. The hot springs will be on the right, though they can be difficult to spot. Look for a small marshy area; the springs and pools themselves are approximately 100 feet beyond, above the river. Start looking for the springs when the river makes a broad meander after 15 crossings. You should also be able to notice the dark green vegetation growing near the springs.

The other route to the springs is longer and more difficult: An 8-mile hike from the visitor center, up the Middle Fork of the Gila River (past the Middle Fork Hot Springs), can also take you to Jordan. Because of the many stream crossings on this journey, however, it is much slower than the one described above.

This is not a hike you will want to do in one day. If you take this route, just keep an eye out for Little Bear Canyon coming in from the left, and look for the hot spring another 2 miles up the canyon.

THE HOT SPRINGS

Jordan is one of the better backcountry hot springs in the West. A series of small warm springs feed into a rock pool that is deep and wide enough to accommodate several bathers. There are actually two pools at the hot springs, one immediately adjacent to the river and ringed by rocks forming a small pool, and the other a larger pool under

GILA CLIFF DWELLINGS

Make sure you take some time to visit the Gila Cliff Dwellings National Monument on your trip to the Gila Wilderness. These two-story structures were occupied by the Mogollon culture and were quite elaborate when built a thousand years ago. Adolph Bandelier, the famed southwestern archaeologist, visited the ruins of the dwellings in 1884, describing them as follows:

Perfectly sheltered, and therefore quite well preserved, the cave villages are perhaps larger than the open air ruins, compactness compensating for the limitation in space. The buildings occupy four caverns, the second of which toward the east is ten meters high. The western cave communicates with the others only from the outside, while the three eastern ones are separated by huge pillars, behind which are natural passageways from one cave to the other.

To reach the cliff dwellings, drive north on NM 15 from the visitor center for 1.5 miles to the parking lot and trailhead. Park here and pick up the 1-mile trail to the cliff dwellings themselves, which are set overlooking the West Fork of the Gila River.

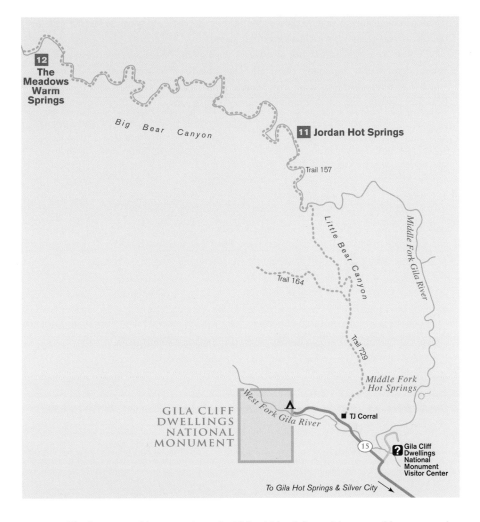

The Meadows Warm Springs

Big Bear Canyon

Jordan Hot Springs

Trail 157

Little Bear Canyon

Middle Fork Gila River

Trail 164

Trail 729

Middle Fork Hot Springs

West Fork Gila River

TJ Corral

GILA CLIFF DWELLINGS NATIONAL MONUMENT

Gila Cliff Dwellings National Monument Visitor Center

To Gila Hot Springs & Silver City

a tree. The larger pool is approximately 25 by 15 by 3 feet with a gravel bottom, and contains beautifully clear water. The temperature in the pool is generally in the mid-90s, making it ideal after a long hike. The setting is also superb, located along the Middle Fork of the Gila River and surrounded by rather lush vegetation. The one-way distance to the springs is approximately 6.5 miles, requiring numerous river crossings. This hike is not recommended for a one-day trip. To really enjoy the hot springs, I recommend that you backpack to them and stay a night or two.

Despite its remote location, Jordan is rather well known and frequently visited, especially during summer months. Do not expect to have the pool to yourself. Whatever you do, be sure to check in at the visitor center for information on water levels and other access issues. Also be sure to notify someone of when and where you are going, and when you are expected back. Don't make this trip if water levels are high or if storms threaten. Trail conditions can be treacherous in wet weather, and flash floods can be deadly in several places along the trail, particularly in the last 0.5 mile of the Little Bear Canyon, which is extremely narrow.

There are several other hot and warm springs in the Gila Wilderness, and you could spend weeks exploring them all. The Meadows Warm Springs are located another 4 miles upstream along the Middle Fork of the Gila River, and the Middle Fork Hot Springs are approximately 8 miles downstream.

12. THE MEADOWS WARM SPRINGS

General description: This extremely remote collection of warm springs in the Gila Wilderness of the Mogollon Mountains requires a long hike of more than 12 miles to reach. There are no bathing opportunities.

Location: Southwestern New Mexico in the Gila Wilderness, near the town of Gila Hot Springs

Primitive/developed: Primitive. There has been no development of the warm springs at all.

Best time of year: Summer and early fall. The warm springs are located high in the Mogollon Mountains, along the Middle Fork of the Gila River, and are only accessible when water levels on the river are low. Do not attempt the trip during periods of high water.

Restrictions: The springs are within the Gila Wilderness, which means motorized vehicles are not allowed. Otherwise, there are no restrictions.

Access: A 12-mile hike (one way) is required to reach the warm springs. The last 7 miles of this route require walking in and out of the Middle Fork of the Gila River.

Water temperature: The source is approximately 91 degrees.

Nearby attractions: Jordan Hot Springs; Gila Hot Springs; Middle Fork Hot Springs; Gila Cliff Dwellings National Monument

Services: There are no services at the warm springs themselves. The most basic necessities (gas and some groceries) can be found at Doc Campbell's, approximately 2 miles from the trailhead. Lodging and showers are also available through the Gila Hot Springs Ranch. More complete services are two hours (40 miles) away in Silver City.

Camping: Undeveloped camping is permitted within the wilderness area, and there are many good places to camp along the way. There are several forest service campgrounds near the Gila Cliff Dwellings National Monument and a small campground at Gila Hot Springs with pit toilets and water. Private campgrounds nearby include Wildwood Hot Springs and Gila Hot Springs RV Park.

Maps: USGS Gila Hot Springs and Woodland Park quadrangles (1:24,000 scale)

For more information: Gila National Forest, Wilderness Ranger District; www.fs.usda.gov/gila; (575) 536-2250; or the Gila Visitor Center in the national monument; www.nps.gov/gicl/planyourvisit/visitorcenters.htm; (575) 536-9461

Finding the spring: From Silver City, travel north out of town on NM 15 to Pinos Altos. Continue on NM 15 through Pinos Altos for approximately 39 miles toward the Gila Wilderness. Drive through the small town of Gila Hot Springs, following signs for the Gila Cliff Dwellings National Monument, and stay on NM 15 for 2 miles. Stop at the visitor center for up-to-date information on river levels and access issues, then go back toward the Gila Cliff Dwellings. About 1 mile from the intersection with the road to the visitor center, you will see a parking area for TJ Corral. Turn right here, and park at the trailhead.

Take Trail #729 (Bear Canyon Trail) north (uphill). At 0.25 mile in, turn right and stay on Trail #729. You will climb almost 1,000 feet on this trail in the first 2 miles, before reaching the summit at the intersection with Trail #164 (Meadows Trail) on your left. Continue straight on Trail #729, which will then descend into the narrow drainage of Little Bear Canyon. The trail intersects Trail #157 (Middle Fork Trail), which you will take to the left (you are now 4.5 miles from TJ Corral).

Trail #157 follows the river, and numerous crossings are required from here on. Hike for about 2 miles upstream, crossing the river 15 times to Jordan Hot Springs. From Jordan Hot Springs, continue up the Middle Fork of the Gila River for another 5.5 miles and 39 river crossings. The Meadows Warm Springs can be difficult to find; watch for a large meadow and a pond fed by warm spring water along the west bank of the Middle Fork of the Gila River. Be sure to bring along a topographic map when making this remote journey. See map on p. 33.

THE HOT SPRINGS

The Meadows Warm Springs are located in an even more remote area of the Gila Wilderness, and are less frequently visited than Jordan Hot Springs. Part of the reason for this, however, is the lack of bathing opportunities afforded by the Meadows. The springs are basically seeps of warm water that feed a small pond not suitable for bathing. The setting is fantastic, however, and is one of the most lush in the wilderness. A large meadow is just beyond the warm springs, affording a very pleasing environment that supports a great deal of wildlife.

Be sure to check in at the visitor center for information on water levels and other access issues. Also be sure to notify someone of when and where you are going, and when you are expected back. Don't make this trip if water levels are high or if storms threaten. Flash floods can be deadly in several places along the trail.

13. TURKEY CREEK HOT SPRINGS

General description: Another remote hot spring in the Gila Wilderness of the Mogollon Mountains, Turkey Creek requires a difficult drive and hike to reach. Several fantastic bathing opportunities await you after the slow drive and 4-mile hike, however. Storms over the past several years, particularly after recent fires, have altered the pools significantly.

Location: Southwestern New Mexico in the remote Gila Wilderness, near the small town of Cliff

Primitive/developed: Primitive. There has been no development of the hot springs at all.

Best time of year: Summer and early fall. The hot springs are located in the Mogollon Mountains, along Turkey Creek, which is a tributary of the Gila River. This area is only accessible when water levels are low. Do not attempt this trip during periods of high water.

Restrictions: The springs are located within the Gila Wilderness. This basically means no motorized vehicles.

Access: The route to the trailhead for Turkey Creek Hot Springs follows a long and sometimes difficult dirt road for approximately 9.5 miles from where the pavement ends. High clearance is required, and four-wheel drive is recommended. From the trailhead, a 4-mile hike (one way) is required to reach the hot springs. The majority of this hike is in and out of Turkey Creek, making it a long journey.

Water temperature: The source is approximately 165 degrees, though there are several pools of varying temperature in which to enjoy the springs, including both hot and warm ones.

Nearby attractions: Brock Canyon Hot Springs; San Francisco Hot Springs

Services: None at the hot springs. Gas and food can be found in the small towns of Gila and Cliff, though only the most basic services are available. More complete services (including lodging) are approximately 40 miles away in Silver City.

Camping: Undeveloped camping is permitted within the wilderness area. There are several nice places to camp near the hot springs, though none are developed (no toilets, water, etc.).

Maps: USGS Canyon Hill and Canteen Canyon quadrangles (1:24,000 scale)

For more information: Gila National Forest, Silver City Ranger District. (505) 388-8201; www.fs.fed.us/r3/gila/about/distmain.asp?district=silver

Finding the spring: From Silver City, head northwest out of town on US 180 for approximately 25 miles to NM 211 (on the right, or east) toward the town of Gila. After 4 miles, bear right on NM 153, as NM 211 bears left. (From the north on US 180, turn left on NM 293 in the small town of Cliff. Bear right on NM 211, then left on NM 153.) Continue on NM 153 (which will turn into NM 155) for 4 miles until the pavement ends, and follow this road for another 9.5 miles. On some maps, this road is labeled Turkey Creek Road. After 1 mile, signs will indicate the end of the county-maintained road. Generally, the road is passable by most high-clearance vehicles (though four-wheel drive is recommended), but during wet weather it can be impassable. The road will go up and over a mountain, following the contours until it reaches Brushy Canyon, where it descends until it departs the canyon and heads up to the right. Just stay on the main road to the right, and soon you will see the Gila River off to your left. As the road descends from here, it crosses a canyon and creek where several undeveloped campsites are located. This is Brock Canyon. Continue on the main road for approximately 1 more mile to its end at a small parking area at the Gila River. Park and begin your hike.

From the parking area, follow the Lower Gila River Trail (#724) upstream. The trail is more like a road (and is often marked by vehicle tracks) for the first mile as it goes in and out of the Gila River several times. Cross the river three times before reaching Turkey Creek and the Turkey Creek Trail (#155) on the left. Turkey Creek will sometimes be dry where it reaches the Gila River. Just follow the main trail up the creek. It passes several old buildings and a windmill in less than 0.25 mile; go through an opening in a stock fence. The trail will soon cross Turkey Creek, which may have water in it at this point. Follow the trail up Turkey Creek for 2 miles to the intersection with Skeleton Canyon, where you bear right, staying in Turkey Creek. The Skeleton Canyon

Trail heads uphill out of the canyon almost immediately, so you know you have gone the wrong way if you find yourself on this trail. Stay to the right in the Turkey Creek drainage.

The last mile of the route to the hot springs is the slowest and most difficult part. Although there are several trails heading upstream, you are pretty much on your own in finding a route. You will have to ford the creek, wade through large pools, scramble under a rock overhang, and go up and over several rock obstacles to make the journey. After about 1 mile, keep an eye out for small trails on your right climbing over a rock obstacle. You may see algae growth as well as greener vegetation, indicating the presence of the springs. You will have to hunt around in this area to find the springs seeping into the creek. There are few obvious rock-lined pools, but you should be able to feel the water temperature changes brought on by the hot water mixing with the creek water. During drier periods there is generally a large 8-foot-deep pool that makes for great swimming. Other pools are frequently washed out. There are several places to camp both upstream and downstream of the hot springs.

THE HOT SPRINGS

The Turkey Creek Hot Springs are not easy to reach and can be difficult to locate, which keeps most casual visitors away. For those looking for a challenging hike and a little bit of hot spring hunting, this place is fantastic. Although the hot springs themselves are high in temperature (165 degrees), they are obscured by Turkey Creek itself. Rock-lined pools are occasionally built in the creek bed to trap the hot water, but they are frequently washed out. Previously, there was one large swimming hole with substantial amounts of hot spring seepage, making the temperature quite warm. With recent flooding, made much worse by fires, the pools have been altered significantly and are in need of reconstruction. Perhaps by the time you make the trip they will be. Soaking pools will vary depending upon what volunteers have built prior to your arrival, but you can usually count on some type of pool or tub. Despite their remote

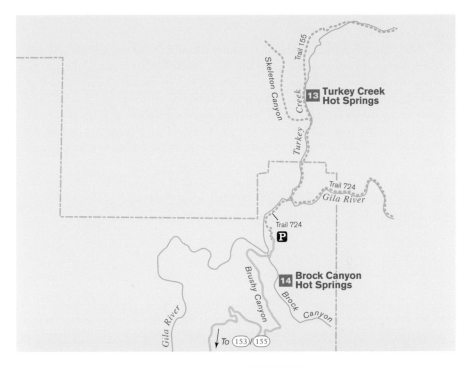

A good view of a large bend in the Gila River can be had from the road, which continues at the top right of the photograph.

location, Turkey Creek Hot Springs are rather well known, so don't expect to have them to yourself.

Make this trip in the late summer or early fall only. Other times of the year can be treacherous, with high water levels and flash floods. Whatever you do, be sure to contact the Gila National Forest for road and trail conditions. I also recommend that you backpack this trip, instead of trying to do it in one day. You may find yourself frustrated by not having enough time. The 4-mile distance is deceiving, as the hike takes much longer than expected due to the frequent river and creek crossings required. Be sure to let someone know when and where you are going, and when you are expected back.

14. BROCK CANYON HOT SPRINGS

General description: This collection of several hot springs in a remote canyon near the Gila River is on the road to Turkey Creek Hot Springs.

Location: Southwestern New Mexico on the margin of the Gila Wilderness, near the small town of Cliff

Primitive/developed: Primitive. The only development has consisted of the placement of pipes to collect the hot spring water, and sometimes small rock-lined pools for bathing.

Best time of year: Summer and early fall. The springs are located in the Mogollon Mountains, and the access road is difficult and occasionally impassable during wet weather.

Restrictions: None. The springs are located within the Gila National Forest.

Access: The hot springs are accessed by a long, difficult dirt road where high clearance is required and four-wheel drive is recommended. A short walk may be required to reach the springs, depending upon road conditions.

Water temperature: Temperatures in the pools vary. Several are warm (90 degrees), while others are hotter (108 degrees).

Nearby attractions: Turkey Creek Hot Springs; San Francisco Hot Springs

Services: None at the hot springs. Gas and food can be found in the small towns of Gila and Cliff, though only the most basic services are available. More complete services (including lodging) are approximately 40 miles away in Silver City.

Camping: Undeveloped camping (no toilets, water, etc.) is permitted at the hot springs.

Map: USGS Canyon Hill quadrangle (1:24,000 scale)

For more information: Gila National Forest, Silver City Ranger District; (505) 388-8201; www.fed.us/r3/gila/about/distmain.asp?district=silver

Finding the spring: From Silver City, head northwest out of town on US 180 for approximately 25 miles to NM 211 (on the right, or east) toward the town of Gila. After 4 miles, bear right on NM 153 as NM 211 bears left. (From the north on US 180, turn left on NM 293 in the small town of Cliff. Bear right on NM 211, then left on NM 153.) Continue on NM 153 (which will turn into NM 155) for 4 miles until the pavement ends, and follow this road for another 9.5 miles. On some maps, this road is labeled Turkey Creek Road. After 1 mile, signs will indicate the end of the county-maintained road. Generally, the road is passable by most high-clearance vehicles (though four-wheel drive is recommended), but during wet weather it can be impassable.

The road will go up and over a mountain, following the contours until it reaches Brushy Canyon, where it descends until it departs the canyon and heads up to the right. Just stay on the main road to the right, and soon you will see the Gila River off to your left. The main road will continue to the left. Bear right here, and as the road descends, it crosses a canyon and creek where several undeveloped campsites are located. This is Brock Canyon. Turn right and follow the canyon upstream for approximately 0.25 mile. If the road is washed out, you may have to park and walk the short distance.

Several collections of hot springs are found in this small canyon, and the first you will come across is approximately 100 yards from the road. You will find a small warm pool beneath some cottonwoods on a bench above the creek. Continue up the canyon and you will reach another pool, also under cottonwoods, though hotter than the first. A third pool was recently washed out in the early 2000s. See map on p. 39.

THE HOT SPRINGS

Brock Canyon Hot Springs consists of a collection of several sources of both warm and hot water in an isolated canyon near the Gila River. Until recently, pipes placed into the hot spring sources concentrated the flow of the water into small pools, ideal for bathing. The lower collection of springs is actually warm and forms a small pool that is not really big enough for bathing. The middle springs' pool was completely washed out during storms, and now all that remains is the pipe itself. This may change in the future, however, if volunteers rebuild a pool or tub. The upper springs are the hottest, and come out of the ground through a pipe at about 108 degrees. The water is collected in a rock-lined pool (5 by 4 by 2 feet), where it is an ideal 99 degrees, perfect for bathing.

Several undeveloped campsites used to be in this canyon, all of which were accessible by vehicle, but the road (as well as the canyon in general) have been periodically flooded and altered by high water. The springs, however, are all within easy walking

The upper hot spring in Brock Canyon provides the best bathing.

distance from the main road to the Gila River. Because of its relative accessibility, Brock Canyon Hot Springs, which used to be not all that well known, is a popular destination.

To get to the Turkey Creek trailhead, continue on the main road past this wash for another mile to the parking area.

RIO GRANDE REGION

The first Europeans to journey into what is now New Mexico arrived via the Rio Grande in the early 1500s, following the river through the dry southwestern portion of the state. When Santa Fe was made the capital of the new Spanish territory, travelers from Mexico City passed through this region, again following the Rio Grande. The river is literally a lifeline through this arid land. There are two collections of hot springs listed for this region, one being the historic Radium Springs and the other consisting of the town of Truth and Consequences, with its numerous small hot spring resorts and spas. I-25 passes north–south through this region, with several towns of note along its length. Las Cruces, Truth or Consequences, and Socorro are the largest communities in the area, though numerous small towns can also be found. A wealth of history, wildlife, outdoor recreation, and scenery awaits the traveler to this region.

Except for Radium Springs, all of the springs in this section are in the town of Truth or Consequences. Truth or Consequences is unique in many ways, beginning with its name. It was originally Hot Springs (for obvious reasons), but in 1950 the townspeople agreed to change its name when the then-popular radio (later television) show offered free publicity to any city that renamed itself Truth or Consequences.

FORT SELDEN

Established in 1865 along the banks of the Rio Grande to protect nearby settlements and travel along El Camino Real, this adobe fort initially housed one company of infantry and one of cavalry. Settlers in the Mesilla Valley had been prey to attacks from Apaches, and the nearby fort was to afford some level of protection for them as well as for travelers along El Camino Real de Tierra Adentro, which at that time was vital to Spanish, Mexican, and American trade and communications.

After the Civil War, troops from the 125th Infantry Regiment were stationed at Fort Selden. These black troops were referred to as "Buffalo Soldiers" by Native Americans because of their short curly hair and indomitable fighting spirit. The fort was abandoned in 1878, only to be reoccupied in 1881, at which time it was reconstructed. Douglas MacArthur lived at the fort for a short time while his father was its commander in the late 1880s. Meanwhile, El Paso had developed into an important railroad town, and nearby Fort Bliss was chosen for expansion. As a result, Fort Selden was ordered closed. Its last troops left in 1887, and its land was given to the US Department of the Interior in 1890.

The property then passed into private hands. In 1963 the fort was donated to the state of New Mexico. The site was declared a state monument in 1974, and restoration work on the adobe buildings began. Recently, the fort has been the location of several experimental adobe restoration practices. Several agencies have been involved with the preservation efforts, including the Getty Conservation Institute.

The monument is open Wed through Mon from 8:30 a.m. to 5 p.m. For more information, contact Fort Selden State Monument, PO Box 58, Radium Springs, NM 88054; (505) 526-8911; www.nmstatemonuments.org.

Prehistorically, the hot springs were revered by both the Mimbres Indians and the later-arriving Apaches. Originally, the springs created a large marshy, muddy area along the Rio Grande. The Apaches believed in the hot springs' curative properties and assigned spiritual significance to them, and no warfare reportedly took place at the springs themselves. The great leader Geronimo was said to have spent considerable time enjoying the springs.

The Spanish called the springs Ojo Caliente de Las Palomas (Hot Springs of the Doves). As white settlers moved in, the river was dammed, channelized, and eventually moved, and soon a town grew up around the springs themselves. With the construction of Elephant Butte Dam, beginning in 1911, many workers arrived. To service these workers, bars and dance halls emerged near the dam site, at a town that became known as Palomas Hot Springs. Soon thereafter Palomas was dropped from the name. During the 1930s hot spring establishments began to emerge in the town. Because of the Great Depression, however, these facilities were simple, no-frills resorts. In its heyday the town contained twelve hot spring resorts and hotels, but as the popularity of such resorts began to wane following World War II, Truth or Consequences went through a steady decline in business activity.

Many of the hot spring resorts fell into disrepair over the ensuing decades, but today "T or C" is in the midst of change. Business is picking up, with a great deal of real estate sold and property changing hands. Many of the old resorts have been or continue to be bought up by both locals and outsiders. A great deal of restoration and rehabilitation work has been going on, bringing several abandoned and closed resorts back online. Despite this, T or C still retains its individuality and charm. The downtown area is free of the usual chain stores and restaurants, and has witnessed the opening of new eateries and art galleries. Best of all, most of the hot mineral bath facilities retain their original buildings and names.

For more information about the hot springs in Truth or Consequences, contact each establishment separately or contact Truth or Consequences and Sierra County Recreation and Tourism (see Appendix B).

15. RADIUM SPRINGS

General description: This historic hot spring resort lies along the Rio Grande in southern New Mexico. Closed for years, recent owners have been trying to open it to the public after years of painstaking rehabilitation. The status of the resort is still up in the air as of this writing.

Location: Southern New Mexico, outside of the small town of Radium Springs, near I-25 north of Las Cruces

Primitive/developed: Developed. The hot water at this location has been harnessed for many years.

Best time of year: The resort plans on being open year-round. Fall, winter, and spring are generally the best times of the year, however, as summers can be rather hot.

Restrictions: This is a private resort, generally requiring reservations.

Access: The resort can be reached via a paved road, as well as a short section of dirt road in the process of being improved.

Water temperature: The source is approximately 129 degrees, while temperatures in the pools vary (104 degrees in the main outdoor pool).

Nearby attractions: Fort Selden

Services: Gas and food can be found in the small town of Fort Selden, immediately off the interstate. More complete services can be found in Las Cruces, approximately 25 miles to the south.

Camping: There is no camping at Radium Springs. A state campground is located at nearby Leasburg Dam State Park.

Map: New Mexico state highway map

For more information: Contact Radium Hot Springs Inn or Doña Ana County; www.donaanacounty.org

Finding the spring: From Las Cruces, travel north on I-25 for approximately 15 miles to exit 19 at Leasburg Dam Road. Exit here and head west. Turn right at the first road, Tel High Road, and make an immediate right turn onto Desert Edge Road. This road parallels the interstate and curves around a large water tower, with the name changing to De Beers Road after approximately 0.75 mile. Turn left at the next T intersection, continue a short distance, and bear right as the road heads into a wash. This section of road is a little sandy but is generally passable by most vehicles. After a short distance, turn left to go under the railroad trestle. Soon after passing under the trestle, turn right into Radium Springs resort.

An easier access road was previously open through Leasburg Dam State Park, but has been closed for several years. Hopes are that this route will soon be available again.

THE HOT SPRINGS

A hotel, bed-and-breakfast, and restaurant—as well as several indoor and outdoor pools—have been in the process of being reopened to the public for years. The most recent owners, who purchased the property in 1995, have been hard at work rehabilitating the resort, undoing damage caused by years of neglect and abuse. By all appearances, it seemed that the resort would soon be a wonderful place to visit. A variety of unfortunate events have occurred to slow the reopening down, however. One of the

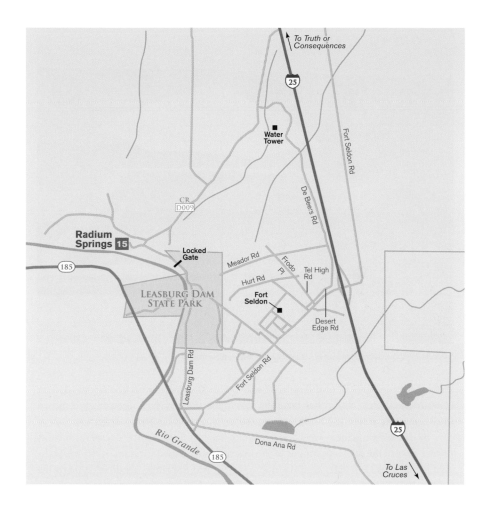

partners passed away, and it seems every possible bureaucratic roadblock that could be placed in the way of the owners has been used. The reason for this opposition is not clear.

Radium Springs, located in a strategic place on an important southwestern travel route, has a rich history. Native Americans knew about the hot springs for centuries. The Apaches considered the springs sacred, and it is reported that their famous leader Geronimo camped here. The springs were discovered by whites as they moved into this part of the country following the Rio Grande. Spanish conquistadores stopped at the springs before they headed east through the dreaded Jornada del Muerto (Route of the Dead). In 1865 the US Army built Fort Selden on the banks of the Rio Grande, and soldiers from the fort partook of the hot mineral water. The springs were then made a part of the military reservation and called Selden Springs, with the first bathhouse built in 1887. The Atchison, Topeka & Santa Fe Railroad was completed through the area in the 1880s, and the big steam engines stopped at the springs to fill up with

Several new outdoor pools have been built at Radium Springs.

water. With the arrival of the railroad and eventual construction of a Harvey House (restaurants, hotels, and other facilities developed for travelers along many railroad lines beginning in the 1870s), the springs received a great deal more attention.

By 1890 Fort Selden was no longer necessary, and the military reservation was turned over to the US Department of the Interior and opened for homesteading. Stanley Llewelyn and his wife were the first to settle at the springs, acquiring title to the land in 1916. The Fort Selden Hot Springs Resort, National Spa Improvement Company was formed to improve the springs and build a resort. In 1917 Selden Springs became known as Radium Springs, and a post office was established. The most well-known resort, however, was constructed by Harry Bailey in 1931. Bailey, who was a friend of New Mexico luminaries Billy the Kid and Pat Garrett, constructed a bathhouse and hotel at the site, and it became known as Bailey's Baths. At that time visitors could access the hotel via NM 28, crossing the Rio Grande at a bridge built in 1926, directly in front of the hotel. In 1935 Valley Road, which became NM 185, was completed, crossing the river on the bridge in front of Radium Springs.

Following decline in the 1940s and 1950s, the property fell into disuse. In 1966 the bridge burned down and was never replaced, leaving the springs isolated. The next occupant was the state of New Mexico, who leased the property for use as a women's prison beginning in 1979. This minimum-security prison was short-lived, however, and the state left in 1983. Another resort was soon attempted by the Daily family, and a Hungarian restaurant was even included as part of the reopening of Radium. A swimming pool along with several individual hot tubs and steam baths were all developed. Nevertheless, the resort was not successful, and was essentially abandoned until the current owners came along in 1995.

In 2000 a gate was installed across NM 28, blocking the main access to Radium Springs. This has left the resort even more isolated, as the only access road includes several hundred feet of sand as well as a narrow, low railroad undercrossing. The current owners have been working hard to get the last remaining portion of the road improved, which will allow them to open to the public.

The historically significant Radium Springs resort was close to completion. The owners have carefully restored the hotel building, which includes a dining area, kitchen, bar, meeting rooms, and original post office. Upstairs are twenty original bedrooms, some with private bathrooms and others with shared baths. Adjacent to the hotel building is the bathhouse, which contains several indoor tubs dating from circa 1931. These are separated into men's and women's sections, with five tubs each. Temperature in these tubs can be regulated by the user by adding cold water. Each of these tubs has been carefully restored to their original appearance. These areas were clothing-optional. Outside are two tubs, with future plans for a third. These tubs were also rebuilt, and provided a fantastic bathing environment. The buildings surround a beautiful patio where parties and special events were held. Finally, a gazebo on the side of the hill provides a wonderful view of the resort and the surrounding country. Unfortunately, all this may be for naught if the owner cannot overcome the variety of bureaucratic challenges.

16. RIVERBEND HOT SPRINGS

General description: A unique hot mineral bath establishment sits on the banks of the Rio Grande, offering private and communal hot pools as well as overnight accommodations.

Location: In the town of Truth or Consequences, southern New Mexico

Primitive/developed: Developed. Riverbend has a casual feel with rustic charm.

Best time of year: Year-round, though summers can be rather hot

Restrictions: This is a private establishment open to visitors for day use as well as overnight guests. Reservations are not necessary but are recommended for overnight accommodations.

Access: The resort is located within the town of Truth or Consequences.

Water temperature: The hot water is brought up from a well at approximately 109 degrees, but cools off to between 95 and 108 degrees in the various tubs.

Nearby attractions: Elephant Butte Reservoir, other Truth or Consequences hot springs

Services: Riverbend offers accommodations. Gas, food, and other lodging can be found within the town of Truth or Consequences.

Camping: Riverbend offers RV camping. Ample camping opportunities are also available at the nearby Elephant Butte Lake State Park.

Map: New Mexico state highway map

For more information: Riverbend Hot Springs; (575) 894-7625; riverbend hotsprings.com

Finding the spring: From I-25 traveling north, take exit 75 and continue toward downtown T or C. Stay on Broadway to Austin Street, where you turn right. Follow Austin Street for 7 blocks to Riverbend on your right. From I-25 traveling south, take exit 79 and follow Date Street for 1.5 miles to Third Street, where you turn left. Go for 1 block, and turn right on Cedar. As the road curves right, you will see Riverbend on the left as the road name changes to Austin. Riverbend is located at 100 Austin St.

THE HOT SPRINGS

Described as containing a "meditative, zen-like" ambience, Riverbend is one of the more unusual establishments in town. While most of the others are contained within bathhouses, Riverbend's baths are outside, open-air, located on the banks of the Rio Grande. There are eight common pools, each with a different temperature. The temperature ranges between 95 and 108 degrees. The first three are named the Hot Minnow Baths, and two are the newer Riverside Rock Pools.

Riverbend has evolved from a youth hostel, to a resort and spa, to a modern though rustic hot springs establishment. The hot mineral water is drawn from the ground and pumped into several tubs overlooking the river. The original tub consists of three pools that were used as bait tanks by the previous owner. These have been converted into baths, with the temperature ranging from 107 degrees in the first, 106 in the second, and finally 105 in the third. The tubs are filled daily with fresh water.

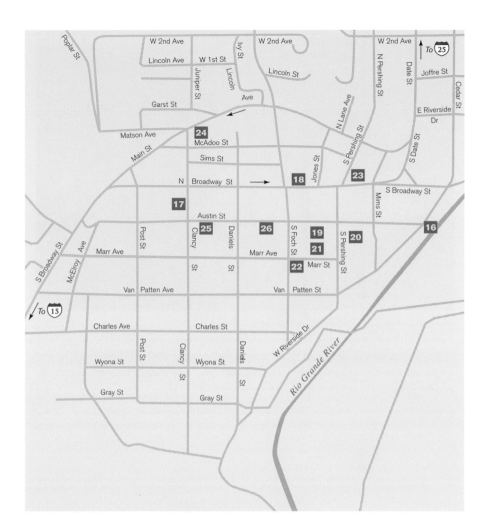

There are also several newer private pools. Bathing suits are required in all of the tubs except for the private ones, where clothing is optional.

Children under twelve are only allowed in two of the private fenced pools, and parents must be present. Otherwise, the grounds are reserved for adults to maintain a quiet, meditative setting. The resort has been upgraded and modernized over the past several years, though still maintains a casual, peaceful feeling.

The resort is open daily from 8 a.m. to 10 p.m., except for pool cleaning from 10 a.m. to 3 p.m. (usually on Thurs). Rates for use of the tubs vary, with fees levied for a one-hour pass offering access to all the common pools, and per person for the classic private pool and for the deluxe private pool. Riverbend also offers overnight accommodations, recommended for couples looking for a quiet retreat. Rooms are rustic, though all have been upgraded and include bathrooms, air conditioning, flat-screen TVs, wireless Internet, and kitchenettes (full kitchens in some). Accommodations

Riverbend offers a private tub where clothing is optional.

range from rooms in the historic courtyard building to several private casitas nearby. There are also RV spots available. The tubs are free to overnight visitors (except the private tubs, which are available at a discounted rate).

17. CHARLES MOTEL AND SPA

General description: This historic motel has hot mineral baths.

Location: In the town of Truth or Consequences, southern New Mexico

Primitive/developed: Developed. The motel and bathhouse are no-frills, with a historic feel and a rustic charm.

Best time of year: Year-round, though summers can be rather hot

Restrictions: This is a private establishment open to visitors for day use as well as overnight guests. Reservations are recommended for overnight accommodations.

Access: The resort is located within the town of Truth or Consequences.

Water temperature: The hot water is brought up from a well at approximately 113 degrees, though temperatures vary from 110 to 112 degrees in the bathhouse.

Nearby attractions: Elephant Butte Reservoir; other Truth or Consequences hot springs

Services: The Charles offers 20 apartment-style rooms (with kitchenettes) in the motel. Gas, food, and other lodging can be found within the town of Truth or Consequences.

Camping: There is no camping at the Charles, but there are plenty of campsites at nearby Elephant Butte Lake State Park.

Map: New Mexico state highway map

For more information: Charles Motel and Spa; (575) 894-7154; charlesmotel andhotsprings.com

Finding the spring: From I-25 traveling north, take exit 75 and continue toward downtown T or C. Stay on Broadway as it becomes a one-way street, continuing to Clancy Street. The Charles is located at 601 Broadway, on the corner of Clancy and Broadway. From I-25 traveling south, take exit 79 and follow Date Street to downtown. As the road curves through downtown, it will turn into Main Street and eventually become a one-way road. Stay on Main to Clancy, where you turn left and proceed to the Charles (on the corner of Clancy and Broadway). See map on p. 51.

THE HOT SPRINGS

The Charles Motel and Spa is one of the oldest continuously operating bathhouses in Truth or Consequences. Established in the 1930s by Charles Lockhart, the motel and bathhouse have not changed much. They retain a distinct style from that era, and prices have risen very little since that time.

The original Charles Apartments were built in the 1930s, followed by the spa building, which was constructed in the 1940s. With many upgrades over the recent years, the Charles Spa now boasts individual hot springs baths, outdoor tubs, detoxifying sweat wraps, massage therapy, reflexology, and conferences. The bathhouse contains a total of nine original tubs, with new ceramic and tile, and is divided into men's and women's sides, though couples can share a single tub. Each side contains several private tubs. Hot water is drawn from depth and can be mixed with cold water to create the ideal bath temperature, depending upon the taste of the bather. There are also two outdoor Jacuzzi tubs located on the roof with views of the surrounding area. All the tubs are drained and cleaned between bathers.

Two modern Jacuzzis like this are in place on the rooftop at the Charles Motel.

The lobby for the motel and bathhouse contains an art gallery and gift shop with wares from many local artists. The bathhouse is generally open from 8 a.m. to 9 p.m. every day. Hourly rates are charged for the baths, and a per-person rate for the rooftop Jacuzzi. The Charles Apartments are available for either short-term or longer-term stays for a fee. Rooms include one or two beds, TVs, full baths, and some contain a full kitchen. Overnight guests are allowed one bath per day.

18. FIRE WATER LODGE

General description: This hot mineral bathhouse is set in a historic motor court.

Location: In the town of Truth or Consequences, southern New Mexico

Primitive/developed: Developed. The motel and bathhouse are casual, with a rustic feel.

Best time of year: Year-round, though summers can be rather hot

Restrictions: This is a private establishment open to overnight guests only (no day use). Reservations are recommended.

Access: The resort is located within the town of Truth or Consequences.

Water temperature: The hot water is brought up from the ground at approximately 112 degrees and ranges between 106 and 110 in the tubs.

Nearby attractions: Elephant Butte Reservoir; other Truth or Consequences hot springs

Services: Fire Water offers a variety of private overnight accommodations, including rooms in the motor court, a casita, and a cottage. All have their own private hot water tubs. Gas, food, and other lodging can be found within the town of Truth or Consequences.

Camping: There is no camping at Fire Water, but there are plenty of campsites at nearby Elephant Butte Lake State Park.

Map: New Mexico state highway map

For more information: Fire Water Lodge; (575) 740-0315; www.firewater lodge.com

Finding the spring: From I-25 traveling north, take exit 75 and

Several private historic concrete baths are available at Fire Water Lodge.

continue 2.7 miles into downtown T or C. Stay on Broadway through town; Fire Water will be on the left at 311 Broadway. From I-25 traveling south, take exit 79 and follow Date Street to downtown. After 1.7 miles the road becomes one way and the name changes to Main Street. Turn left at Foch Street, then left again at the next stop sign at Broadway, and proceed to Fire Water on the left. See map on p. 51.

THE HOT SPRINGS

Fire Water Lodge is a hot mineral water establishment set in a motor court dating back to the 1950s. It still retains its historic charm, with several individual rooms set around a garden courtyard. Each room comes with its own private hot mineral water tub (some indoor and some outdoor). Tubs consist of concrete, ceramic tile, stone, and metal. There is also a new outdoor hot water soaking tub in a private area with shade cover. Tubs are only available to overnight guests. There are several private rooms, as well as a larger casita and a cottage. All rooms have Wi-Fi, air conditioning, a microwave, a refrigerator, etc., and a range of rates apply. A variety of spa services are also available with advance notice. Fire Water, like many of the resorts in Truth or Consequences, is very reasonably priced and has a casual, rustic feel. It's best to call ahead as rates are subject to change.

19. LA PALOMA TOO HOT SPRINGS (HAY-YO-KAY HOT SPRINGS)

General description: This historic bathhouse offers six private pools and tubs, all fed by their own hot artesian water sources.

Location: In the town of Truth or Consequences, southern New Mexico

Primitive/developed: Developed, with a casual environment

Best time of year: Year-round, though summers can be rather hot

Restrictions: This is a private establishment open to visitors for modest use fees.

Access: The resort is located within the town of Truth or Consequences.

Water temperature: The hot water is brought up from a natural artesian source at approximately 110 degrees, and ranges between 100 and 108 degrees in various tubs and pools. Water temperatures vary slightly depending upon the season.

Nearby attractions: Elephant Butte Reservoir; other Truth or Consequences hot springs

Services: La Paloma Too offers two two-bedroom condos for rent, both with complete kitchens. Gas, food, and other lodging can be found within the town of Truth or Consequences.

Camping: There is no camping at La Paloma Too, but there are plenty of campsites at nearby Elephant Butte Lake State Park.

Map: New Mexico state highway map

For more information: La Paloma Too Hot Springs; (575) 894-2228; www .lapalomahotspringsandspa.com

Finding the spring: From I-25 traveling north, take exit 75 and continue toward downtown T or C. Stay on Broadway headed east. Follow Broadway to Austin Street, where you turn right. Follow Austin for several blocks to La Paloma Too at the corner of Austin and Pershing (300 Austin St.). Traveling south on I-25, take exit 79 and continue on Date Street into downtown. Stay on Date Street as it becomes one way and the name changes to Main Street, and turn left on Pershing Street. Continue to La Paloma Too at the corner of Pershing and Austin. See map on p. 51.

THE HOT SPRINGS

Formerly known as Hay-Yo-Kay, La Paloma Too is the oldest continuously operating bathhouse in town, with the existing bathhouse built in 1920. It is also one of the few in town to be fed completely by a natural hot artesian source with no pumping required, as opposed to the hot wells in most of the other facilities. There are six pools and tubs, and each is fed by its own hot-water source, which constantly recirculates the water (about every twenty to thirty minutes). Temperatures in the pools vary seasonally, but generally range from 100 to 108 degrees. There are five sandy-bottomed private tubs in the main bathhouse, with varying temperatures. A bigger pool is located in the Long House adjacent to the main bathhouse, and it is ideal for larger groups. The tubs are open to the public for day-use soaking Mon through Thurs, 7 a.m. to noon and 5 p.m. to 11 p.m.; Fri through Sun 7 a.m. to 11 p.m. Call ahead for reservations.

There is a large pool in the Long House at La Paloma Too.

A fee is charged per person per half hour for the indoor and the outdoor pool; group rates are available. There are two two-bedroom condos available for rent, which include full kitchens as well as complimentary soaking in the tubs during your stay. Massage services are also available. Reservations are recommended for the condos as well as the massage services.

20. **INDIAN SPRINGS**

General description: A historic motel and bathhouse features two small private pools fed by natural hot artesian water.

Location: In the town of Truth or Consequences, southern New Mexico

Primitive/developed: Developed, with a rustic charm

Best time of year: Year-round, though summers can be rather hot

Restrictions: This is a private establishment, though the baths are available for day use for a fee. Baths are free for those staying in the motel.

Access: The resort is located within the town of Truth or Consequences.

Water temperature: The hot water is approximately 110 degrees as it comes out of the ground, cooling to 105 or 106 degrees in the pools.

Nearby attractions: Elephant Butte Reservoir; other Truth or Consequences hot springs

Services: There are six motel units available for rent, either nightly or monthly. Gas, food, and other lodging can be found within the town of Truth or Consequences.

Camping: There is no camping at Indian Springs, but there are plenty of campsites at nearby Elephant Butte Lake State Park.

Map: New Mexico state highway map

For more information: Contact Indian Springs; (578) 894-2018

Finding the spring: Indian Springs is located across the street from La Paloma Too at 218 Austin St. From I-25 traveling north, take exit 75 and continue toward downtown T or C. Stay

The private tubs at Indian Springs have a rustic charm with gravel bottoms.

on Broadway headed east to Austin Street, where you turn right. Follow Austin for several blocks to Indian Springs. Traveling south on I-25, take exit 79 and continue on Date Street into downtown. Stay on Date Street as it becomes one way and the name changes to Main Street, and turn left on Pershing Street. Continue to Indian Springs at the corner of Pershing and Austin. See map on p. 51.

THE HOT SPRINGS

Indian Springs consists of a small historic motel and bathhouse with two private pools. Like La Paloma Too, Indian Springs is fed by a natural artesian spring, with no need for pumping. Each sandy-bottomed pool is separate and private, and is available for rent for thirty minutes at a time. A small bath can accommodate one to two people, and the larger can fit up to six people. Water temperatures vary depending upon the season, but are generally 105 to 106 degrees. Pools are available to those staying in the motel, which currently has six units for overnight or monthly accommodations. Those staying in the rooms can have two free half-hour baths per day. Day use is also welcome on a walk-in, first-come-first-serve basis between 8 a.m. and 9 p.m. daily. Rates are charged per person per half hour.

Indian Springs has been owned by the same family for more than 25 years and has a quiet, historic charm to it. Originally established in the 1930s, the current owners have maintained the "old-time" feel of the motel and bathhouse, and have ensured that it has remained a nice place to stay and enjoy the hot artesian water. Hours are 7 a.m. to 11 p.m. Call ahead for rates.

THE SPACEPORT

In case Truth or Consequences needed another reason to be considered unusual, it can now boast of being home to a new spaceport 23 miles to the southeast. The state of New Mexico apparently plans to spend millions of dollars over the next several years to build what is to be called the Southwest Regional Spaceport.

In late 2005 billionaire entrepreneur Sir Richard Branson (founder of Virgin Records, Virgin Atlantic, and Virgin Mobile) announced his plans to lease the spaceport for his Virgin Galactic space tourism missions. He plans to launch Spaceship Two from the 27-square-mile facility, which is located just west of the White Sands Missile Range. Virgin Galactic plans to take 10,000 passengers per year into space, and apparently more than 38,000 people have already paid (or put a deposit down for) the $200,000 for the trip. Flights were expected to begin in 2008, but obviously that has not happened yet.

Many believe this facility will become the center of a growing commercial space-travel industry. This would give Truth or Consequences, which is the closest town to the facility, a great deal of exposure, leading to new businesses and jobs.

21. LA PALOMA HOT SPRINGS & SPA

General description: This historic motor court and bathhouse has a variety of accommodations and pools utilizing natural artesian water.

Location: In the town of Truth or Consequences, southern New Mexico

Primitive/developed: Developed, with a historic and rustic charm

Best time of year: Year-round, though summers can be rather hot

Restrictions: This is a private establishment open for day use as well as overnight guests. No children under 7 allowed in the pools or pool rooms.

Access: The resort is located within the town of Truth or Consequences.

Water temperature: The hot water emerges from the ground at approximately 116 degrees and ranges between 98 and 116 in the various pools.

Nearby attractions: Elephant Butte Reservoir; other Truth or Consequences hot springs

Services: La Paloma offers several rooms for rent in its historic motor court, each with its own kitchen.

Gas, food, and other lodging can be found within the town of Truth or Consequences.

Camping: There is no camping at La Paloma, but there are plenty of campsites at nearby Elephant Butte Lake State Park.

Map: New Mexico state highway map

For more information: La Paloma Hot Springs; (575) 894-3148; www.la palomahotspringsandspa.com/en-us

Finding the spring: From I-25 traveling north, take exit 75 and continue toward downtown on Broadway. Turn right on Pershing, and proceed for 1.5 blocks. Go right on Marr Street to the main entrance at 311 Marr. If traveling south on I-25, take exit 79 and continue for 3 miles into downtown. Continue on Date Street as it becomes one way and the name changes to Main Street. Turn left on Foch Street and proceed to the first stop sign at Broadway. Turn left on Broadway and proceed 1 full block to Pershing, where you turn right, and travel 1.5 blocks. Go right on Marr to the main entrance. See map on p. 51.

THE HOT SPRINGS

Formerly known as Marshall Miracle Pools, La Paloma has been undergoing an extensive upgrade and improvement process. The resort is fed by a natural hot artesian source (like only a few other establishments in town), so no pumping is required. This allows for a constant recirculation in all of the pools. The pools themselves are located in an old bathhouse adjacent to the motel rooms, and have sandy bottoms and water temperatures ranging between 98 and 116 degrees.

La Paloma is built around an old motor court that actually dates to the construction of the Elephant Butte Dam. Small cabins lived in by workers who built the dam were moved to Marshall after the completion of the dam. Once there they were converted into a motor court. Today the property harkens back to the heyday of automobile travel in the 1930s, '40s, and '50s. Each of the rooms has been refurbished, while maintaining the historic feel of the motor court. There is a variety of types of rooms, each with a kitchenette or full kitchen, along with two room suites complete with

The owners of La Paloma Hot Springs have maintained the historic charm of the original motor court.

dining rooms, kitchens, and living rooms. All overnight guests receive complimentary use of the pools.

The water is described as "structured" or "living" water, which means the water flows naturally without any pumping required. The bathhouse is built over a hot mineral drainage canal. There are numerous pools, all fed by this natural artesian water. All are in private rooms, where clothing is optional. One outdoor communal pool is available, where suits are required unless reserved for private soaking. Fees are charged per person per half hour or per hour for use of the indoor pools. An outdoor, private pool is also available for a fee per person per half hour and per hour. La Paloma is open every day from 10 a.m. to 6 p.m.

22. ARTESIAN BATH HOUSE AND RV PARK

General description: This small bathhouse and RV park offers several private indoor tubs.

Location: In the town of Truth or Consequences, southern New Mexico

Primitive/developed: Developed, with a rustic and historic feel

Best time of year: Year-round, though summers can be rather hot

Restrictions: This is a private establishment, open for day use as well as to those staying in the RV park.

Access: The resort is located within the town of Truth or Consequences.

Water temperature: The hot water is brought up from the ground from an artesian well at approximately 112 degrees, cooling to about 108 in the tubs.

Nearby attractions: Elephant Butte Reservoir; other Truth or Consequences hot springs

Services: Gas, food, and lodging can be found within the town of Truth or Consequences.

Camping: RV camping is available at Artesian by the day, week, or month. There are also plenty of campsites at nearby Elephant Butte Lake State Park.

Map: New Mexico state highway map

For more information: Artesian Bath House and RV Park; https://sites.google.com/site/artesianbathhousenm/Home; (575) 894-2684

Finding the spring: From I-25 traveling north, take exit 75 and continue on Broadway toward downtown. Stay on Broadway to Foch Street and turn right. Follow Foch for 2 blocks to Marr Avenue and turn left. Artesian is located at 312 Marr. From I-25 traveling south, take exit 79 and follow Date Street to downtown. Continue on Date Street as it becomes one way and the name changes to Main Street. Turn left on Foch Street and follow it for 2 blocks to Marr Avenue, then turn left to 312 Marr. See map on p. 51.

THE HOT SPRINGS

Artesian is small historic bathhouse with an associated RV park. It has changed little since originally opening in 1930, and has been in the same family for more than twenty-five years. The hot water is drawn from an artesian well and diverted into a total of eight private baths. There are five individual tubs and three larger baths that can hold several people. Pool temperatures are generally 108 degrees. Fees are charged per hour per person or per bath. A daily fee is charged for RV hookups. The bathhouse is open daily from 8 a.m. to noon and 1 to 5:30 p.m., with extended hours until 9 p.m. on Fri, Sat, and Sun as well as during the winter months.

23. PELICAN SPA

General description: This bathhouse on the site of an old motor court offers a variety of baths as well as accommodations in several locations.

Location: In the town of Truth or Consequences, southern New Mexico

Primitive/developed: Developed, with a distinct rustic charm

Best time of year: Year-round, though summers can be rather hot

Restrictions: This is a private establishment open for day use as well as overnight guests.

Access: The resort is located within the town of Truth or Consequences.

Water temperature: Temperatures in the tubs range between 104 and 114 degrees.

Nearby attractions: Elephant Butte Reservoir; other Truth or Consequences hot springs

Services: Pelican offers a variety of overnight accommodations in its upgraded motor-court rooms. Gas, food, and other lodging can be found within the town of Truth or Consequences.

Camping: There is no camping at Pelican, but there are plenty of campsites at nearby Elephant Butte Lake State Park.

Map: New Mexico state highway map

For more information: Pelican Spa; www.pelican-spa.com; (575) 894-0055

Finding the spring: From I-25 traveling north, take exit 75 and continue toward downtown on Broadway.

A common area is available to all guests staying at Pelican Spa.

Turn left at Pershing Street. Pelican Spa is located at 306 Pershing, near the corner of Broadway. From I-25 traveling south, take exit 79 and continue on Date Street toward downtown. Continue on Date Street as it becomes one way and the name changes to Main Street. Turn left on Pershing and follow it to the Pelican Spa. See map on p. 51.

THE HOT SPRINGS

Pelican Spa is one of the newer spas in town, built from a 1930s motor court known as Cozy Corners. After much rehabilitation work, Pelican Spa now offers private hot mineral water baths as well as accommodations in a wide variety of refurbished historic rooms. There are five private mineral springs baths, four tubs accommodating two people and a fifth that can fit up to six bathers. Accommodations are available in the main bathhouse as well as in the adjacent motel complex. Each of the rooms are different, and many contain a sitting room and kitchenette. One of the rooms in the main bathhouse has its own private hot mineral bath. All overnight guests have free, unlimited use of the tubs in the bathhouse. Walk-in use of the tubs is also welcome, with fees for half an hour or per hour. A common area with a kitchen, washer, and dryer is also available to overnight guests. Prices for rooms are reasonable, whether in the motel complex or for larger rooms. A variety of spa services are available at Pelican, as well as the Studio de La Luz, adjacent. Call ahead for up-to-date rates.

24. SIERRA GRANDE

General description: This luxurious spa and bathhouse on the site of an old apartment building offers a variety of hot mineral water experiences.

Location: In the town of Truth or Consequences, southern New Mexico

Primitive/developed: Developed. Sierra Grande is by far the most lavish of the bathhouses in Truth or Consequences.

Best time of year: Open year-round, though summers can be rather hot

Restrictions: This is a private establishment open for day use as well as overnight guests.

Access: The resort is located within the town of Truth or Consequences.

Water temperature: The water is 112 degrees as it emerges from the ground. Temperatures in the baths range between 107 and 112 degrees.

Nearby attractions: Elephant Butte Reservoir; other Truth or Consequences hot springs

Services: Sierra Grande offers numerous rooms in the completely renovated lodge building. Gas, food, and other lodging can be found within the town of Truth or Consequences.

Camping: There is no camping at Sierra Grande, but there are plenty of campsites at nearby Elephant Butte Lake State Park.

Map: New Mexico state highway map

For more information: Sierra Grande; sierragrandelodge.com; (877) 288-7637

Finding the spring: From I-25 traveling north, take exit 75 and go east on Broadway into downtown. Turn left on Foch Street, then left on McAdoo Street. Sierra Grande is located at 501 McAdoo. From I-25 traveling south, take exit 79 and follow Date Street into downtown as it becomes one way and turns into Main Street. Turn left on Foch Street, then right on McAdoo. See map on p. 51.

THE HOT SPRINGS

Built on what was an apartment building dating to 1929, Sierra Grande is the most lavish spa in town. Purchased by Ted Turner in 2013, the resort is now one of his "Ted Turner Expeditions" offerings. As with previous owners, the current owner has spared no expense in making Sierra Grande a luxurious retreat. The property centers on the lodge building, which was formerly apartments and then went through several machinations before being virtually abandoned. This building was completely refurbished, with numerous pools and spa rooms added. Hot mineral water is drawn from a well that provided the first commercial baths in town (prior to the construction of the apartments) and is diverted into several pools. These are all modern, beautifully built pools, both indoor and outdoor, each available for half-hour rental (which includes use of a shower, towels, and fresh ice water). The resort is in the process of developing other portions of the grounds for additional bathing experiences, most of which will be outdoors. All guests staying overnight at Sierra Grande are allowed a complimentary private soak each day of their stay.

Sierra Grande also offers a plethora of treatments (massages, facials, wraps, and reflexology, among others) and is committed to the continuing education of its

Each of the rooms at Sierra Grande contains a large spa-type bathtub.

therapists, so much so that it is converting an old hotel building at the top of the hill into an educational facility. A portion of the treatment area is located in what was once a bar, Rocky's, attached to the apartment building.

Accommodations are provided in the lodge building and have been completely refurbished, each with its own sunken tub as well as unique theme. These are by far the most upscale rooms in town, and include the use of the mineral baths as well as a continental breakfast. A private casita with its own private mineral bath is also available. Finally, the resort contains a gourmet restaurant, with a well-known chef at the helm. Sierra Grande is quite a place, and quite different from the other bathhouses in town. There are plans for further expansion and improvements over the next few years.

Both the indoor and outdoor tubs are available for day use between 7 a.m. and 10 p.m. Fees are levied for a half hour, and if no one is waiting the owners often let you stay longer. Water is provided, as are towels.

25. HOOSIER HOT SPRINGS

General description: This relatively new hot spring bathing establishment in Truth or Consequences offers three outdoor and one indoor baths open for day use.

Location: In the town of Truth or Consequences in southern New Mexico

Primitive/developed: Developed, though casual in feel

Best time of year: Year-round, though summers can be hot

Restrictions: Hoosier is a private establishment, open for day use only.

Access: Hoosier is located in the town of Truth or Consequences.

Water temperature: Water is 112 degrees as it emerges from the ground, and baths range between 107 and 112 degrees.

Nearby attractions: Elephant Butte Reservoir; other Truth or Consequences hot springs

Services: Hoosier is available for day use of the hot tubs only. Gas, food, and other lodging can be found within the town of Truth or Consequences.

Camping: There is no camping at Hoosier, but there are plenty of campsites at nearby Elephant Butte Lake State Park.

Map: New Mexico state highway map

For more information: Hoosier Hot Springs; (575) 740-6096

Finding the spring: Hoosier is located at 516 Austin. If coming from the north, take exit 79 from I-25 in Truth or Consequences. Bear right as the road becomes Date Street. Go through the first traffic light and continue 2 miles to the second light, Continue on Date Street as it bends to the right and becomes Main Street (one way) downtown. Follow Main as it curves and goes up a hill. Turn left at Clancey, go 4 blocks to Austin Street, and turn left to reach the spa.

From the south, take exit 75 for Williamsburg and Truth or Consequences. You will be on South Broadway Street, which you follow through Williamsburg for a couple of miles. Broadway will becomes one way as it enters downtown. Turn right on Austin Street to Hoosier. See map on p. 51.

THE HOT SPRINGS

Hoosier Hot Springs is another recently restored historic hot springs establishment from the heyday of Truth or Consequences. The small, rustic establishment contains three outdoor baths and one indoor bath. Rates are charged per couple per hour or per half hour. The spa is open from 1 p.m. to 8:30 p.m. or by special appointment.

Hoosier Hot Springs is in a notable building in the Truth or Consequences Historic District. The Hoosier Apartments were built in 1937 in an architecturally distinctive style, reflecting elements of the Territorial Style, but also retaining its own uniqueness. The apartments were built by Harold and Jen Lotz, who came to New Mexico from Indiana. Lotz and his wife initially settled in Santa Fe, and took the waters at Ojo Caliente, seeking their health benefits. The couple moved to Hot Springs in 1937, purchasing property and hiring a local contractor to construct the apartments Harold designed himself. An artesian well was drilled on-site, which was used to fill several tiled baths as well as a concrete lap pool. Later, during the 1950s, additional rooms were constructed at the back of the apartments.

26. BLACKSTONE HOTSPRINGS

General description: A newly renovated hot spring bathing establishment in Truth or Consequences offers overnight accommodations in a retro-themed motor court, and day use of several different private hot spring baths.

Location: In the town of Truth or Consequences in southern New Mexico

Primitive/developed: Developed, though casual in feel

Best time of year: Year-round, though summers can be hot

Restrictions: Blackstone is a private establishment, with baths open to overnight and day-use guests.

Access: Blackstone is located in the town of Truth or Consequences.

Water temperature: Water is 110 to 112 degrees as it emerges from the ground, though bath temperatures can be controlled by adding cold water to your preference.

Nearby attractions: Elephant Butte Reservoir; other Truth or Consequences hot springs

Services: Blackstone contains overnight accommodations as well as hot tubs. Gas, food, and other lodging can be found within the town of Truth or Consequences.

Camping: There is no camping, but there are plenty of campsites at nearby Elephant Butte Lake State Park.

Map: New Mexico state highway map

For more information: Blackstone Hotsprings; (575) 894-0894; www .blackstonehotsprings.com

Finding the spring: Blackstone is located at 410 Austin Street. If coming from the north, take exit 79 from I-25 in Truth or Consequences. Bear right as the road becomes Date Street. Go through the first traffic light and continue 2 more miles to the second light. Continue on Date Street as it bends to the right and becomes Main Street (one way) in downtown. Follow Main as it curves and goes up a hill. Turn left at Foch Street (at the El Cortez Theater sign), and go 3 blocks to Foch and Broadway. Stay on Foch Street to Austin Street (the next stop sign). Turn right on Austin Street to Blackstone, which is on the left in the middle of the block.

From the south, take exit 75 for Williamsburg and Truth or Consequences. You will be on South Broadway Street, which you follow through Williamsburg for a couple of miles. Broadway becomes a one-way street as it enters downtown. Turn right onto Foch Street, then right on Austin Street to Blackstone. See map on p. 51.

THE HOT SPRINGS

Blackstone is a recently renovated 1930s-era motor court turned into a modern hot springs establishment, with distinct homage paid to the 1940s and 1950s. The motor court was in shambles before the current owners completely refurbished it in 2005–2006. Blackstone offers both overnight accommodations and day use. There are a total of six private baths, including the Red Bath, Yellow Bath, and Turquoise Bath (which are outdoor), and the indoor Wet Room, which contains a hot spring tub for soaking as well as steam rooms and a waterfall shower. These rooms are all large and

TRUTH OR CONSEQUENCES

Truth or Consequences is one of the most interesting towns in the state, particularly if you are a hot water enthusiast, but also if you appreciate historic buildings and a slower pace. Geologically speaking, the town is also fascinating. The water table is close to the surface, where it is heated by magma at depth, and the water rises along a fault line along the Magdalena limestone ridge that divides the city (you can pick out this ridge, or "hogback," by looking for the city's water tank).

Prior to 1907, the Rio Grande River ran to what is about Main Street today. A flood in that year caused the channel of the river to change to more or less its current track. So, historically there were only a couple of hot springs (such as Geronimo or Government Springs) visible to those passing through the area, while most geothermal activity was underwater. With the completion of Elephant Butte Dam in 1916, the current channel of the Rio Grande was established. At that point, because the water table was so close to the surface, hot water began to flow in the area of what is now the center of the bathhouse district.

Several early bathhouses drew from this water, including Indian, Hay-Yo-Kay, and Marshall—the only ones that can be considered truly free-flowing. Other resorts came along and utilized artesian water sources and wells for baths. In the late 1800s, the area was known as Palomas Hot Springs, and a few modest bathhouses emerged. With the construction of Elephant Butte Dam in the 1910s, many people came to the area, and discovered the plentiful thermal mineral waters.

Between 1911 and 1916, a large number of dam workers were housed nearby, bringing a ready demand for businesses in the town 5 miles away from the dam site. The town grew quickly and was incorporated in 1916, as it gained a reputation as a health resort. Of course, this was a time when "taking the waters" was an accepted curative process.

Eventually the town's name was changed to Hot Springs, and finally to its current name in 1950. The popular radio show of the same name invited any town in the country to change its name to that of the show, which city leaders, boosters, and the chamber of commerce saw as a good opportunity for publicity and a good way to differentiate the place from other hot springs towns. Residents voted to approve the name change on March 31, 1950.

Many residents came to the town from the Midwest, so it reflects their tastes and styles. Many buildings were also moved from the dam project to be repurposed in the town. A variety of distinctive architectural styles were used by these people, including bungalows, as well as a variety of revival styles including Spanish Revival, Mission Revival, and Territorial Revival. Thankfully, the town still retains many buildings from this period, some with only minor modifications. The central core of this business district is listed on the National Register of Historic Places for this reason.

luxurious. There are also two historic baths consisting of restored bathtubs in private rooms. Water temperature is approximately 110 to 112 degrees from the ground, varying in each room. Cold water can be added to cool off the hot water if needed.

Baths are open for day use for fifty minutes per session. There are also numerous rooms for lodging, each with a different retro theme and most with their own hot spring bath. The springs are open from 9 a.m. to 9 p.m. Mon through Thurs; 9 a.m. to 10 p.m. Fri through Sun. Children under twelve are not allowed.

NORTHERN
NEW MEXICO

The upper pool at Spence Hot Springs offers excellent bathing.

JEMEZ SPRINGS AREA
(SANTA FE NATIONAL FOREST)

The Santa Fe National Forest is blessed with countless hot and warm springs sprinkled throughout. The area around Jemez Springs is particularly rich in geo-thermal resources. For hot spring enthusiasts in New Mexico, this is one of the best areas for a natural experience. Many of the hot springs are privately owned, but there are plenty that are on forest service land and open to public use. Several of the springs described below require a hike to reach them. Although this does provide for a more rustic experience, most are rather well known, and you can expect to share them with others.

The Santa Fe National Forest also offers beautiful scenery, along with a multitude of outdoor activities such as fishing, hiking, camping, and backpacking. The area is serviced by the hamlet of Jemez Springs, as well as the larger town of Los Alamos to the west. Be sure to visit the Jemez State Monument when in the town of Jemez Springs.

Before visiting the springs in the area, contact the Santa Fe National Forest's Jemez Ranger District for weather, access, and other information.

27. SPENCE HOT SPRINGS

General description: A collection of natural hot springs is on the side of a steep hill forming several soaking pools in a beautiful setting. Heavily visited for years, Spence has had somewhat of a notorious reputation of overuse, trash, and partying. Despite this reputation, efforts by the forest service to protect the area have improved it somewhat.

Location: Northern New Mexico, approximately 32 miles west of the town of Los Alamos, within the Santa Fe National Forest

Primitive/developed: Primitive. The only improvement consists of the construction of several rock pools; otherwise, the springs are in a pristine state.

Best time of year: Open year-round, though roads may be closed at times during winter. Fall and spring are the best times to visit.

Restrictions: The forest service manages the springs, and the agency's rules should be obeyed. These include no nudity, no glass, no fires, and day use only. Dogs are permitted, but must be on leash. The parking lot is designed to accommodate only seven cars to discourage overuse. No parking is permitted along the highway. When the parking lot is full, there is overflow parking available at the Dark Canyon Fishing Access, 0.25 mile to the north.

Access: The springs are located a short hike off a paved highway.

Water temperature: The source is approximately 106 degrees. Though considered by many to be more of a warm spring, temperatures in the pools vary, and generally hover around 95 degrees in the largest and most popular.

Nearby attractions: The surrounding Santa Fe National Forest offers a multitude of attractions. There are also several other springs in the vicinity, including McCauley Warm Springs, Jemez Springs, Soda Dam, Jemez Hot Springs, and San Antonio Hot Springs.

Services: Gas, food, and lodging can be found in the small community of Jemez Springs, 6 miles to the south. For more extensive services, Los Alamos is 32 miles to the east.

Camping: Camping is not permitted at Spence Hot Springs, nor in the parking lot. There are several forest service campgrounds in the area, however.

Map: USGS Los Alamos quadrangle (1:100,000 scale)

For more information: Santa Fe National Forest, Jemez Ranger District; (575) 829-3535; www.fs.usda .gov/santafe

Finding the spring: From Los Alamos, travel west out of town on NM 4 for approximately 30 miles to NM 126 at La Cueva Lodge. Continue on NM 4 for another 1.4 miles to a large parking area on your left (between mile markers 24 and 25). From Jemez Springs, travel north on NM 4 for approximately 6.5 miles to the parking area on your right. At the parking lot, look for a trailhead at the south end. The well-maintained trail begins with a series of steps and then switchbacks down to and across the San Antonio River on a new bridge. On the other side of the bridge, the trail is not quite as well maintained, but just follow the most well-worn path that leads uphill. This trail is steep, and several smaller trails branch off from it. Just stay on the main trail up the hillside to the springs. You will eventually encounter the overflow from the hot springs, which you can follow to the pools themselves. The hike is about 0.25 mile long.

THE HOT SPRINGS

A very popular hot springs, Spence usually has several people partaking, and once you get there, you'll see why. There are many sources of hot and warm water on the hillside, forming several bathing pools. Two of the largest pools are set among large boulders and contain sandy bottoms. The water has reportedly decreased in temperature over the past several years, and is approximately 95 degrees in the most popular pool, so it's not very hot. It also appears that the flow has decreased, as several former pools are dry now. A small cave nearby contains much warmer water that flows out into the pools. A small waterfall was located beneath the lower of these pools, forming a small pool itself. From these main pools, you could continue uphill, following the water and a small trail. There were several other pools tucked away on the hillside, overlooking the magnificent countryside.

Spence has had a long and varied history. For years it was a favorite hangout for a variety of characters. Because of lack of enforcement, many of these people remained at the hot springs for long periods of time, some even building shelters. Following some unsavory conduct and several complaints, the forest service attempted to regulate the springs to a greater degree. As a result, visitation is permitted only during daylight hours.

Because of its popularity, Spence is once again suffering from overuse. Trash is common on the trail and at the hot springs themselves. Although the forest service officially prohibits nudity, and claims that rangers will cite you if you are found in that condition, they have for the most part allowed it to continue, as long as there are no problems or complaints. Do not be surprised to find some going nude at Spence.

A wide variety of people visit Spence, and it is rare to have the area to yourself. If you are seeking solitude and peace, you might want to try another nearby spring, such as San Antonio or McCauley. I also highly recommend you avoid this hot spring on weekends, and instead focus on weekdays, or at least early in the morning.

Please help to keep this location open by obeying posted signs and not littering. If problems persist at Spence, there is a chance the forest service will close all public access, which would be a shame.

28. MCCAULEY HOT SPRINGS

General description: This is another collection of spectacular natural hot springs in the Jemez Springs area, with several large pools of warm water perfect for bathing.

Location: Northern New Mexico, approximately 35 miles west of the town of Los Alamos, within the Santa Fe National Forest

Primitive/developed: Primitive. The only alteration has been the creation of several rock dams to trap the hot spring water in pools for bathing.

Best time of year: Year-round, though trails will be virtually impassable during wet weather in early spring and winter. Roads may also be closed at times during winter. Because these are warm springs, cold weather may also make them somewhat less appealing.

Restrictions: The springs are within the Santa Fe National Forest, and all regulations should be obeyed, which include no nudity and day use only.

Access: A hike of approximately 2 miles one way is required to reach the springs. Because it is uphill most of the way, this can be a somewhat strenuous hike. During wet weather or when river levels are high, the trail may be difficult or even impassable.

Water temperature: The source is approximately 90 degrees, and the water cools as it flows downhill into the various pools. Depending upon the time of year, the water will generally be in the mid 80s.

Nearby attractions: Jemez Falls; Spence Hot Springs; San Antonio Hot Springs; Jemez Springs; Jemez Hot Springs

Services: Gas, food, and lodging can be found in the small town of Jemez Springs, approximately 4 miles to the south. For more complete service, Los Alamos is about 35 miles to the east.

Camping: Camping is not permitted at the hot springs. Backpack camping is permitted 400 feet from the warm springs and 200 feet from the river. There are several forest service campgrounds in the area, including Jemez Falls at the alternate trailhead.

Maps: USGS Los Alamos quadrangle (1:100,000 scale); Jemez Springs and Redondo Peak quadrangles (1:24,000 scale)

For more information: Santa Fe National Forest, Jemez Ranger Station; (575) 829-3535; www.fs.usda .gov/santafe

Finding the spring: From Los Alamos, travel west out of town on NM 4 for approximately 30 miles to NM 126 at La Cueva Lodge. Continue on NM 4 for another 2 miles to the Battleship Rock Picnic Area (past the parking area for Spence Hot Springs). From Jemez Springs, travel north on NM 4 for approximately 4 miles to the Battleship Rock Picnic Area. Pull into the picnic area, head toward the large Battleship Rock, and park.

Cross a bridge and head toward a large gazebo and fireplace area. Behind the gazebo is the trailhead for the East Fork Trail (#137). Follow this trail as it winds its way along the Jemez River. Be sure to stay on the main trail, which has very little in the way of signs along its length. During periods of high water, you may find yourself going up the hillside and back down again to avoid the river.

Hike for 1.75 miles, mostly uphill, until you see a small stream flowing downhill from your left. This is the water from McCauley Hot Springs. Follow this small creek, though there is not a well-defined trail. Hike uphill for approximately 0.25 mile until you reach several pools of water. The largest pool at the top is the source.

Another route is via a 2.5-mile hike from the Jemez Falls Campground. To reach it, travel east on NM 4 for 4 miles from La Cueva Lodge (and the junction with NM 126) to the signs for Jemez Falls. Turn south on this road and proceed past the campground to the parking lot for the falls. Take the trail to Jemez Falls, branching off at the East Fork Trail (#137), and continuing for a little over 2 miles to McCauley Hot Springs. Be sure to view Jemez Falls on your way back (0.25 mile from the split with Trail 137). See map on p. 74.

THE HOT SPRINGS

More accurately described as a warm spring, McCauley is located in a beautiful forest setting, well worth the 2-mile one-way hike to reach. The source bubbles out of the ground on a relatively steep hillside, flowing into a large pond of crystal clear water. From here, the water flows downhill into several other pools created by small dams. Each pool is slightly cooler than the one above it. You will also find small fish in some of the ponds that may gently nibble at your feet. The scenery is fantastic here, isolated and primitive. The rugged volcanic landscape is complemented by a healthy forest environment and the nearby Jemez River.

Despite the sometimes difficult hike along the river, do not expect to have McCauley to yourself. It is a well-known hot spring and is well publicized. On most weekends, you can expect to see others. It appears that both bathing suits and nudity are common at the springs, though official forest service policy prohibits nudity. Be sure to hike only during low water periods of the Jemez River. The trail will be muddy and often impassable during wet weather in the late fall, winter, and early spring.

A day-use fee is levied at the Battleship Rock Picnic Area. The namesake Battleship Rock is an amazing feature, consisting of 200 feet of welded volcanic ash. The formation looks like the prow of a large ship, hence the name. Climbing on the rock is prohibited, but a small trail leads along its margin, with several picnic sites. A footpath continues along the north end of the picnic area, leading you to Hidden Falls, a beautiful site worth seeing.

There are other hot springs in the area, though none are as easy to reach nor provide as good a bathing experience as McCauley. If you are an intrepid hot spring enthusiast, however, these other "secret" hot springs could be the adventure you are looking for.

29. SAN ANTONIO HOT SPRINGS

General description: Yet another fabulous collection of hot springs in the Santa Fe National Forest, these springs flow out of a steep hillside and form several bathable pools.

Location: Northern New Mexico, approximately 40 miles from the town of Los Alamos, within the Santa Fe National Forest

Primitive/developed: Primitive. The only improvement consists of the formation of several rock-lined pools.

Best time of year: Though open all year, the road to the hot springs will be closed to vehicles during winter. The best time to visit is generally late spring, summer, and early fall.

Restrictions: The springs are within the Santa Fe National Forest, and all regulations should be obeyed, which include no nudity and day use only.

Access: A 6-mile drive on a fairly well-maintained dirt road is required, followed by a short climb uphill. The road is closed to motor vehicles during winter. The road can be rough, so a high-clearance vehicle is recommended. If the road is wet, four-wheel drive is mandatory.

Water temperature: The source is approximately 129 degrees. The water cools substantially as it flows downhill into the various pools, though the top one is around 105 degrees.

Nearby attractions: Spence Hot Springs; McCauley Hot Springs; Jemez Springs; Jemez Hot Springs

Services: Gas, food, and lodging can be found in the small town of Jemez Springs, approximately 12 miles to the south. More complete services can be found in Los Alamos, about 40 miles to the east.

Camping: Camping is not permitted at the hot springs, but is allowed in the surrounding area. There are also several developed campgrounds nearby, including La Cueva on NM 4.

Map: USGS 7 Springs quadrangle (1:24,000 scale)

For more information: Santa Fe National Forest, Jemez Ranger Station; (575) 829-3535; www.fs.usda .gov/santafe

Finding the spring: From Los Alamos, travel west out of town on NM 4 for approximately 30 miles to NM 126 at La Cueva Lodge. Turn right on NM 126 and drive for about 3.7 miles to FR 376 on the right. Turn onto the dirt road. The gate may be closed to motor vehicles during certain times of the year (generally in winter). If so, park and walk (or ride a bicycle). This road is generally well-maintained, but can be full of holes after wet weather. Follow the road as it goes through the forest for 6 miles until you reach what looks to be an intersection, and you see a large cabin across the creek to the right. Take the road to the right as it goes downhill and then crosses the creek at a small bridge. Park and follow a faint trail up the steep hillside. You will see the water from the hot springs flowing down the hill. The walk uphill to the springs is less than 0.25 mile, but it is steep.

THE HOT SPRINGS

In a magnificent setting, San Antonio is a must-visit if you are in the Jemez Springs area of the Santa Fe National Forest. Although a 6-mile drive (or hike, bike ride, or horseback ride) on a dirt road is required, the springs are well worth it. Flowing out of a steep hillside, the hot spring water comes out of the ground at about 129 degrees and forms the first of several pools. The springs' source was actually bolstered by the Civilian Conservation Corps (CCC) in the 1930s to ensure a regular flow. The top pool is large and shallow, and is perfect if you want a hot soak. The water then flows downhill into several smaller pools, each one successively cooler. No matter which one you choose, you will have a great view of the surrounding valley, creek, and forest.

Despite the journey required to reach the springs, you can generally expect to find others at this spot, particularly on summer weekends. It appears nudity as well as bathing suits are common at San Antonio Hot Springs, although, as with other hot springs in the area, the forest service prohibits nudity. Be sure to leave plenty of time to hike in and out, and also bring plenty of water.

Like Spence Hot Springs, the forest service has also had problems with San Antonio. Vandalism to the nearby CCC cabin has caused the forest service to limit access in the past. As with other well-known hot springs, San Antonio is experiencing the

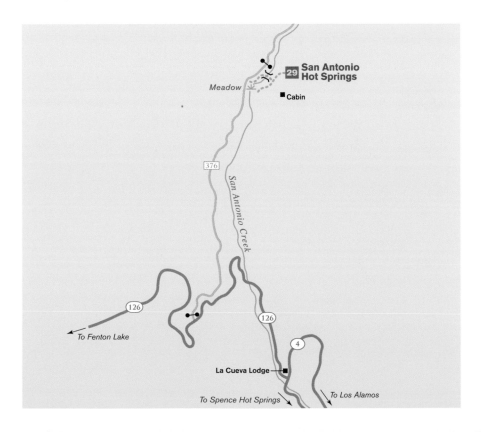

effects of overuse and abuse. Trash has become more common, though conditions are still better than more accessible hot springs. Camping is not permitted, and the springs are only open for day use (6 a.m. to 10 p.m.). Please respect the cabin and the hot spring and do not damage either, ensuring that the area will stay open to the public in the future.

30. **SODA DAM**

General description: A magnificent natural dam has formed in the Jemez River from the precipitation of minerals from a collection of hot springs. Although very limited bathing opportunities are available, Soda Dam is a natural wonder and is located immediately off the main highway, well worth a stop.

Location: Northern New Mexico, 2 miles north of the town of Jemez Springs and approximately 36 miles from the town of Los Alamos

Primitive/developed: Primitive. No improvements have been made to the springs, hence the limited bathing opportunities. A small parking area and interpretive sign are located immediately off the highway next to the dam.

Best time of year: Year-round, though roads may be difficult and occasionally closed during winter storms

Restrictions: The dam is only open for daytime use. Be careful near the edge of the river, as ledges can be slippery and steep.

Access: Soda Dam is located immediately off a paved highway.

Water temperature: The source is approximately 117 degrees.

Nearby attractions: Spence Hot Springs; McCauley Hot Springs; San Antonio Hot Springs; Jemez Springs; Jemez Hot Springs. The Santa Fe National Forest also offers almost unlimited outdoor recreation, including hiking, camping, backpacking, and fishing.

Services: Gas, food, and lodging can be found in the small town of Jemez Springs, 2 miles to the south. For more extensive services, Los Alamos is approximately 36 miles away.

Camping: Camping is not permitted at Soda Dam itself, but several developed campgrounds are in the surrounding Santa Fe National Forest.

Map: USGS Los Alamos quadrangle (1:100,000 scale)

For more information: Santa Fe National Forest, Jemez Ranger Station; (575) 829-3535; www.fs.usda .gov/santafe

Finding the spring: From Los Alamos, travel west out of town on NM 4 for approximately 30 miles to La Cueva Lodge. Continue on NM 4 for another 6 miles; Soda Dam is on the left (east) side of road. From the town of Jemez Springs, travel north on NM 4 for about 2 miles to Soda Dam, on your right. There is a forest service sign immediately before the springs.

THE HOT SPRINGS

A fantastic geologic wonder, Soda Dam was created over hundreds of years by hot mineral water flow. Soda is actually a misnomer, as the deposit is not made of sodium bicarbonate, but instead of travertine. The hot springs precipitated minerals (mostly calcium carbonate) that eventually formed a dam across the Jemez River, constricting its flow at one time. During the construction of NM 4, a portion of the natural dam was removed, but the most dramatic portion of the dam remains immediately to the east of the highway. The river rushes through a small opening in the mineral

The Soda Dam is an amazing geological feature along the Jemez River.

precipitate. Small caves have also been formed by the springs, making for a very interesting site.

This is one of the most geothermally active areas in the Jemez Springs area, as the numerous old travertine deposits attest. Many more hot springs could be found in the area prior to the construction of the highway, which appeared to alter the geothermal system somewhat. There are also rock shelters in the immediate vicinity of Soda Dam, including the famous Jemez Cave. An extensive archaeological deposit was found in the cave during the 1930s, indicating that the area around Soda Dam has been used for well over 2,000 years by a variety of cultures—small wonder when one considers the abundant cold and warm water found at this beautiful location.

There are a variety of hot spring sources in the area of Soda Dam. Several small seeps can be found in the little cave adjacent to the dam. You can also see some other hot springs immediately across the road from Soda Dam. These springs are little more than puddles of warm water, and run along the highway for a short distance. A small pool of warm water is in place at the foot of the dam, immediately above the river. This is not really a great place to bathe, but is interesting nonetheless. A pullout and parking area along with an interpretive sign are the only developed areas around the springs.

Soda Dam is definitely worth a stop when driving along NM 4, and poking around the dam is a pleasant diversion. Take a few minutes to explore and enjoy this geologic wonder, but be careful, as many of the surfaces are slippery.

31. JEMEZ SPRINGS BATH HOUSE

General description: A historic hot mineral bathhouse, Jemez still offers baths the old-fashioned way. Located at the margin of the Santa Fe National Forest in the small town of Jemez Springs, this is a great place to stop for a relaxing bath in a private room.

Location: Northern New Mexico in the hamlet of Jemez Springs, between the Santa Fe National Forest and the Jemez Indian Reservation, approximately 40 miles from the town of Los Alamos and 20 miles from the small town of San Ysidro

Primitive/developed: Developed, with a rustic charm

Best time of year: Year-round

Restrictions: The bathhouse is owned and operated by the town of Jemez Springs and is open to visitors for a small charge. No pets or children under fourteen allowed. No alcohol is allowed.

For more information: Jemez Springs Bath House; www.jemezspringsbath house.com; (575) 829-3303

Finding the spring: From Santa Fe, take US 84/285 north toward Española for approximately 15 miles to NM 502 toward Los Alamos. Head west on NM 502 to Los Alamos (or take NM 4 as a bypass around the town). Continue west on NM 502 (which changes to NM 501) through Los Alamos to NM 4. Turn right on NM 4 (left goes toward Bandelier National Monument), and continue for approximately 30 miles to La Cueva Lodge. Continue on NM 4 for approximately 10 miles (passing Soda Dam) to the town of Jemez Springs. The bathhouse is located in the town's small park, next to a fire station and library.

From Albuquerque, travel north on I-25 for 15 miles to Bernalillo. Take exit 242 and go west on US 550 toward San Ysidro and Cuba. At San Ysidro (about 25 miles), turn right on NM 4 toward Jemez Pueblo, Jemez Springs, and Los Alamos. Continue for 17 miles to Jemez Springs.

THE HOT SPRINGS

Located in an incredibly rich geothermal area, Jemez Springs was named for the hot springs from which the bathhouse gets its water. According to locals, in 1860 settlers in the area heard a roar and witnessed the hot spring erupt like a geyser. Following the eruption, a rock enclosure was constructed around the hot spring, and the water has been used ever since. The bathhouse now standing was constructed sometime in the 1870s (though expanded in the 1940s) and is one of the oldest buildings in the area. It has changed little since that time.

Puebloan peoples have been living along the Jemez River for centuries, undoubtedly using the area's plentiful hot springs. Spanish explorers and missionaries first came to the area beginning in the sixteenth century. Franciscan missionaries built a stone church, named San Jose de Guisewa, in 1622 in an attempt to Christianize the local Native Americans. A small band of Jemez Indians was already living in a community they called Guisewa, which means "place at the boiling waters." Today a state monument marks the place where the Jemez people built their homes. The Spanish,

The Jemez Springs Bath House is located in the small town of Jemez Springs.

however, forced the Puebloans to settle farther down the valley, in the location of the present-day reservation.

During the 1840s, when whites first began to settle in the area, a town called Ojos Calientes emerged around the hot springs. In 1888 the town's name was changed to Archuleta, after the family that built the first bathhouse at the spring a decade earlier. Finally, in 1907, the town's name was changed to Jemez Springs. At the height of the popularity of hot spring resorts, there were two in Jemez Springs, including the one you see today. The current bathhouse was used by the Catholic Church as a retreat for priests in the 1940s and 1950s. In 1961 the property was sold to the town of Jemez Springs, in whose hands it remains today. The bathhouse itself is leased to individuals who operate and run it.

Today you can choose from eight private individual indoor tubs. Hot mineral water is fed directly into the old-fashioned concrete tubs, and because the source water is so hot (169 degrees), cold water is added by the user to get the right temperature. Bathing suits are not required as each room is private. Tubs are sized for single use. There are also a variety of spa treatments available, in addition to massage. The spring itself is located immediately behind the bathhouse in a covered gazebo (built in 1936). The tubs are for individual use; fees are charged for 25 minutes and for 50 minutes. There are also fees for massages, ranging from a half hour to one and a half hours. Towels can be rented for a fee. It is a good idea to phone ahead, particularly for massage services (575-829-3303). Hours are 10 a.m. to 6 p.m. Sun, Mon, Tues; and 10 a.m. to 7 p.m. Thurs, Fri, and Sat. The bath house is closed Wed for cleaning. At one time a large outdoor swimming pool and several cedar hot tubs were available. Unfortunately, they are currently not in use, though this may change in the future.

Several other hot springs are in the area, including one utilized by a Buddhist center adjacent to the Jemez Springs Bath House, Cañon del Rio Retreat & Spa, and Jemez Hot Springs (Giggling Springs) farther down the road. More hot springs can be found along the Jemez River, though none of them provide bathing opportunities. The entire area is geo-thermally active, part of a massive caldera, referred to as a super volcano by some, and commonly known as the Valles Caldera. All hot springs in the immediate area owe their presence to this geologic feature.

32. JEMEZ HOT SPRINGS (GIGGLING SPRINGS)

General description: This outdoor hot spring resort with several pools is located in the small town of Jemez Springs. Though relatively new, Jemez Hot Springs is on the site of the town's oldest hot spring establishment. The property was for sale at the time of this writing.

Location: Northern New Mexico, in the hamlet of Jemez Springs between the Santa Fe National Forest and the Jemez Indian Reservation, approximately 40 miles from Los Alamos and 20 miles from the small town of San Ysidro.

Primitive/developed: Developed, with a casual and friendly feel

Best time of year: Year-round

Restrictions: The resort is privately owned, open to visitors for a small charge. No pets, glass containers, or alcohol are allowed.

Access: The resort is located immediately off the highway, down a short dirt driveway.

Water temperature: The source is approximately 139 degrees, though the temperature in the pool is maintained at between 102 and 104 degrees.

Nearby attractions: Jemez Springs Bath House; Jemez State Monument; Soda Dam; Spence Hot Springs; McCauley Hot Springs; San Antonio Hot Springs

Services: Gas, food, and lodging can be found in the small town of Jemez Springs. More extensive services can be found in Los Alamos, approximately 40 miles away.

Camping: There is no camping at Jemez Hot Springs, but there are several developed campgrounds in the Santa Fe National Forest as well as on the Jemez River south along NM 4.

Map: New Mexico state highway map

For more information: Jemez Hot Springs; (575) 829-9175; www.gigglingsprings.com

Finding the spring: From Santa Fe, take US 84/285 north toward Española for approximately 15 miles to NM 502 toward Los Alamos. Head west on NM 502 to Los Alamos (or take NM 4 as a bypass around the town). Continue west on NM 502 (which changes to NM 501) through Los Alamos to NM 4. Turn right on NM 4 (left goes toward Bandelier National Monument) and continue for approximately 30 miles to La Cueva Lodge. Continue on NM 4 for approximately 10 miles (passing Soda Dam) to the town of Jemez Springs. Go through town and look for a small sign for the resort on the right. The driveway for Jemez Hot Springs (Abousleman Loop) is immediately south of the Jemez Mountain Inn and across the highway from the Laughing Lizard Cafe.

From Albuquerque, travel north on I-25 for 15 miles to Bernalillo. Take exit 242 and go west on US 550 toward San Ysidro and Cuba. At San Ysidro (about 25 miles), turn right on NM 4 toward Jemez Pueblo, Jemez Springs, and Los Alamos. Continue for 17 miles to Jemez Springs, and look for the driveway to Jemez Hot Springs on the left, on the south side of town.

THE HOT SPRINGS

Jemez Hot Springs was formerly known as Giggling Springs, and is the newest hot spring establishment in the area, built on the site of the first bathhouse in the village of Jemez Springs. The owners, who purchased the property in 1995, have put in additional pools, as well as a cabana, pavilion, and shade sailcloths. There are now four pools of differing sizes and temperatures, generally in the 100- to 104-degree range. The original large pool (approximately 17 by 27 feet), like all the pools, is fed by natural hot spring water and lined with natural red sandstone rocks. A patio of flagstone surrounds the pool area. The Jemez River is immediately adjacent to the pools, and several hammocks and chairs are provided for relaxation. Also on the property, immediately next door, are the remains of the oldest bathhouse in town, which operated from the late nineteenth century until 1950. The current owners initially offered cabins for overnight accommodations, but have since focused only on day use.

The owners of Jemez Hot Springs put an emphasis on relaxation, and they achieve it well with their friendliness, as well as the natural and casual feel of their pool and grounds. There is also a cabin with restroom and changing rooms. Swimsuits are required throughout the grounds. Passes are available for a per person fee for one hour, two hours, a half-day, and all day. Though reservations are not accepted, the number of bathers is limited to maintain plenty of room and ensure the relaxation of each user. Be sure to bring a towel, too (towel rentals are no longer available). The small registration building has a gift shop with swimsuits, drinking water, and other

A beautiful pool area awaits you at Jemez Hot Springs.

spring necessities. Hours vary by the season and the day, but are generally 11 a.m. to 7 p.m. during the week and 11 a.m. to 9 p.m. on weekends. Be sure to check the website or call ahead for up-to-date information. The pool can be privately reserved during or after regular hours.

SANTA FE AREA

The tourist capital of the state, Santa Fe provides ample opportunities to experience New Mexico's rich cultural and recreational resources. Founded in 1607, Santa Fe is one of the oldest continually occupied cities in North America. Its long tradition of Native American, Spanish, Mexican, and Anglo roots gives it a distinctive flavor and feel. The original plaza is still in place, surrounded now by art galleries, restaurants, and shops. Despite its growth and popularity, Santa Fe has been able to maintain its connection to the past.

Be sure to visit the Palace of the Governors when you are in the area. Constructed in the seventeenth century by the Spanish, the palace dominated the plaza (and still does today). It withstood the violent revolt of the Pueblo Indians in 1680, and has served as the seat of power for New Spain, Mexico, the Confederate States of America, and the United States. Today the building houses a fantastic museum representing New Mexico's rich history.

Santa Fe also serves as the gateway to many of New Mexico's wilderness areas. The Sangre de Cristo Mountains are a short drive east of the city, where hiking, biking, backpacking, camping, fishing, and, in winter, skiing can be found in abundance. Though there are virtually no natural hot springs in the immediate Santa Fe area, the Japanese-style Ten Thousand Waves spa offers plenty of hot-water alternatives. It is only a short drive into the mountains from Santa Fe.

FORT UNION

Just up the interstate from Las Vegas lie the remains of an old cavalry outpost, Fort Union. Established in the 1860s, Fort Union was located along the strategic Old Santa Fe Trail, connecting settlements in New Mexico and the rest of the Southwest with the western plains and the Midwest. In its heyday, it was the largest fort in the Southwest. Fort Union not only housed several cavalry units, but also served as a depot and arsenal for US military operations over a wide region. It became an important supplier to most of the other army posts in Arizona and New Mexico.

Today Fort Union is the largest collection of adobe ruins in the United States. The National Park Service has been trying to maintain, stabilize, and repair the adobe buildings since the 1950s. Although efforts have not always been successful, the buildings are still in fairly good shape, and give the visitor a feel of what a nineteenth-century military post was like. To reach Fort Union from Las Vegas, travel north on I-25 for 21 miles to exit 366 for NM 161. Head west on NM 161 for about 5 miles to the fort.

33. TEN THOUSAND WAVES

General description: This upscale Japanese-inspired spa and resort is located immediately outside Santa Fe, offering an incredible variety of treatments and bathing options, along with lodging and a restaurant.

Location: Northern New Mexico, a few miles outside Santa Fe

Primitive/developed: Developed. There are actually no natural hot springs at Ten Thousand Waves, but visitors are offered a wide assortment of features and amenities.

Best time of year: Year-round

Restrictions: This is a private establishment, and reservations are requested for all private baths, treatments, and lodging. Walk-ins are accepted for the communal bath, but due to the popularity of the spa, there may not be any availability.

Access: The resort is located a few miles from Santa Fe, on a paved road.

Water temperature: Well water is heated by a gas heater and purified before reaching the tubs, which range in temperature from 104 to 106 degrees.

Nearby attractions: City of Santa Fe; Hyde Memorial State Park; Santa Fe ski area

Services: Gas, food, and lodging can be found in Santa Fe, less than 4 miles away. Lodging is available at Ten Thousand Waves in a variety of different units ranging in price per night.

Camping: There is no camping at Ten Thousand Waves itself, but camping is available in the nearby Santa Fe National Forest.

Map: Santa Fe area map

For more information: Ten Thousand Waves; (505) 982-9304; tenthousand waves.com

Finding the spring: From the plaza in downtown Santa Fe, follow Bishops Lodge Road/Washington Avenue north out of town, past the Scottish Rite Temple, to Artist Road. Turn right on Artist Road and follow it as it turns into Hyde Park Road, with signs for the ski area. Stay on Hyde Park Road for approximately 3 miles to Ten Thousand Waves on your left.

THE HOT SPRINGS

It's only a short drive from Santa Fe, but Ten Thousand Waves is far enough away to give one the sense of seclusion. Labeled a "Japanese health spa," Ten Thousand Waves is far more. Designed to mimic as closely as possible the Japanese "onsen," the resort has made continual upgrades over the past many years. With numerous baths to choose from—plus a variety of massage options, spa treatments, and facials, along with a new restaurant—you could spend days at this location.

Upon entering the main building, the visitor is given a locker for personal belongings and a kimono for wearing around the grounds. Following a shower, there are several bathing opportunities. There are two communal tubs outside, one coed and the other for women only. Swimsuit bottoms are required in the communal tub, known as the Grand Bath. There are a variety of private baths, each with a unique theme and different amenities. Each contains hot tubs and saunas. The premium

The Waterfall Room includes a beautiful hot pool to enjoy.

rooms offer a traditional soaking tub with an open balcony, heated bathroom with shower, sauna, and cold water plunge, and cooling berth. Another contains a warm waterfall complete with warm tub, rock deck, sauna, and cold plunge. The rest of the outdoor tubs are made of wood, concrete, or acrylic, and are secluded enough from each other to provide privacy. All of the tubs have their own saunas, along with changing rooms and showers.

The treatments are too numerous to mention here, but include twenty-one rooms featuring massage, herbal wraps, salt glow, aromatherapy, East Indian cleaning treatments, Watsu, and acupuncture. There are 130 therapists on staff. Those receiving treatments are granted free access to the communal tubs. A wide variety of lodging rooms, including the Zen, Townsman, and Emperor's Rooms, are available for a range of rates per night.

Opened in 1981, Ten Thousand Waves has an interesting history, and was not always received warmly by locals. The property was previously owned by a marijuana grower, who had to dump it quickly. Duke Klauck purchased the property with the idea to open a Japanese-style spa and resort. To meet that end, the grounds were converted to look like a resort in the mountains of Japan, complete with landscaping and bamboo-style construction. The property continues to be updated and improved, with new services being continuously offered.

Ten Thousand Waves is an upscale spa and resort, and is therefore quite a bit more expensive than most other hot spring facilities. Tub rates range for the communal bath to private spa suites, and per-person rates for the most luxurious of the private baths (known as premium). Hours vary depending on season. The high season is generally between mid-May and mid-October, though ski season can also be busy. Reservations should be made ahead of time.

34. MONTEZUMA HOT SPRINGS

General description: A collection of hot springs bubbles out of the side of a hill, feeding a variety of rock and cement tubs. Originally utilized by the historic Montezuma Castle Resort, the springs are now accessible to the public courtesy of the current owners, the United World College.

Location: Northern New Mexico, outside the town of Las Vegas

Primitive/developed: Although the springs were at one time part of a resort, today the tubs lie out in the open, undeveloped. The setting isn't exactly rustic, however, as the springs are located on the side of the road and are now owned by a college.

Best time of year: Year-round

Restrictions: Montezuma Hot Springs is owned by the United World College, which currently allows public access. Bathing suits are required, and the public is not allowed to use the springs between midnight and 5 a.m.

Access: The springs are located immediately off the highway.

Water temperature: The source is approximately 138 degrees, though the tubs are considerably cooler, ranging from roughly 98 to 112 degrees.

Nearby attractions: Fort Union National Monument; Santa Fe Trail

Services: Gas, food, and lodging can be found in Las Vegas, approximately 6 miles away.

Camping: Camping is not permitted at Montezuma, but there are ample camping opportunities in the Santa Fe National Forest to the west.

Map: USGS Montezuma (1:24,000 scale); New Mexico state highway map

For more information: Armand Hammer United World College of the American West; www.uwc-usa.org

Finding the spring: From Santa Fe, travel 64 miles east on I-25 to the town of Las Vegas. In Las Vegas, take exit 65W and cross over to the west side of the freeway. Turn right on Business 25 to Mills Avenue and turn left. Follow Mills for 1.5 miles to Hot Springs Road (NM 65), with signs for Montezuma and the United World College, and turn right. Follow Hot Springs Road for approximately 5 miles to the imposing Montezuma Castle on your right. A little farther on, you will see signs for the hot springs, which are immediately off the road to your right. Park along the road and walk to whichever tub you would like.

THE HOT SPRINGS

A collection of three groups of hot springs have been diverted into rather rustic cement and rock pools and tubs along the side of the road in the small community of Montezuma. Montezuma Castle, as well as several other resorts, originally operated numerous indoor hot spring pools. Most of the bathhouses are gone today, and the hot springs are out in the open. Pools and tubs range in size and temperature, and with a little experimenting, you can find the perfect soak. Although Montezuma Hot Springs are well known, there are plenty of pools to choose from, and with a little patience, you can always get a tub to yourself. The setting is fantastic, as the springs lie along the Gallinas River adjacent to several historic buildings from a bygone era.

Because the owner, the United World College, maintains stringent regulations for using the tubs, they have been kept rather clean, and bathers tend to be orderly. Bathing suits are required, and the pools are closed from midnight to 5 a.m.

Apparently, the name Montezuma was given to the hot springs when a group of soldiers under the command of General Stephen Watts Kearny was marching west during the Mexican War in 1846. In the vicinity of the town of Las Vegas (which was founded in 1821), the troops ran into the Pecos Indians, who maintained the famed Mexican ruler Montezuma was raised at the springs. Their legend stated he was carried back to Mexico by eagles when he was ready to assume the throne.

The Native Americans had been using the springs for centuries, at least since the founding of the Pecos Pueblo in the ninth century. Spanish ranchers moved to the area beginning in the early nineteenth century, although the springs saw little development. Prior to and during the Civil War, a small hospital was erected for ailing soldiers, as was the practice at many hot springs across the country. A modest adobe hotel was eventually built at the springs in the 1870s, but visitation remained relatively slight.

The Montezuma Castle itself was constructed by the Santa Fe Railroad Company in 1885 to serve as a grand hotel. The railroad had reached the area in 1878 and bought the property encompassing the hot springs soon thereafter. Originally the railroad built a small hotel at the site. When it was destroyed by fire, however, the holding company, the Las Vegas Hot Springs Company, decided to build big. A second, larger hotel was constructed, containing 240 rooms, but it was also damaged by fire. Finally, the railroad company decided to build a more permanent facility that would be the wonder of the region.

The castle was designed by world-renowned architects Burnham and Root, who gave the hotel a kind of medieval, storybook quality. The new resort also contained several other buildings to take advantage of the nearby hot springs. The hotel was supplied with steam by a massive power plant nearby (which can still be seen today). Several noted luminaries visited the hotel, including Ulysses S. Grant, William T. Sherman, and Theodore Roosevelt. This hotel building was also damaged by fire, but was partially rebuilt in 1886 and renamed the Phoenix, only to close in 1903. It was later owned by the Baptist Church and then by the Catholic Church, which ran a seminary for Mexican priests there from 1937 from 1972. The castle was then left empty, and it suffered from neglect and vandalism.

In 1981 the Armand Hammer Foundation bought the castle for the United World College, but because of neglect, the mighty building was structurally unsound. In fact, until recently, the Montezuma Castle was on the National Trust for Historic Preservation's 11 Most Endangered Historic Places List. In 1997, however, local support rallied, and funds were gathered to repair and restore the castle. Beginning in 2001, the hotel received a $10.5 million renovation. It now serves as an international center with student and faculty housing, dining facilities, offices, a campus store, and student social center. Tours are provided by the college, free of charge.

As with so many other hot springs, Montezuma has had several issues, including some people using the springs during off-hours, as well as using alcohol and soaking nude. Unfortunately, this may ruin it for the rest of us. Broken glass is found in places from this abuse, and should be watched out for. The college really wants to keep this spring open, but continued misuse will certainly lead to closure. Be sure to pack out all trash, and obey all posted regulations.

Enjoy the hot springs at Montezuma while you soak in the historic feel of this area.

TAOS AREA

Serving as a gateway to fantastic hot spring country, Taos is a destination in itself. With pueblos dating back hundreds of years to a contemporary art scene, Taos is a New Mexico original. Almost unlimited outdoor activities await you in the surrounding countryside, from hiking to downhill skiing. Located close to the Rio Grande, Taos makes a perfect base from which to visit the hot springs of the area. For information on the outdoors opportunities in the area, contact the Carson National Forest; www.fs.usda.gov/carson; (575) 758-6200.

Black Rock and Manby Hot Springs are located in the area of the fantastic Rio Grande Gorge, which runs 90 miles north–south through the northern part of the state. The gorge is part of what is known as the Rio Grande rift, a place where the earth's crust is stretched and magma lies close to the surface. This magma provides the heat for the hot springs. For many years, volcanoes erupted and poured lava over this area, leaving behind the basalt you see today. More recently, the Rio Grande cut through this basalt, forming a canyon, or gorge. The almost perpendicular cliffs of the gorge (more than 1,000 feet in places) have proved an impediment to travel for centuries.

Following the completion of bridges over the river in the early twentieth century, the thriving community of Taos was finally connected to the Denver & Rio Grande Railroad to the west. Interestingly, two of these bridges were constructed close to Black Rock and Manby, and the hot springs were undoubtedly part of the plans for development of the area. Unfortunately—or fortunately—there was never any lasting development of either of the springs, due to their rugged location, as well as their isolation.

The Rio Grande provides a variety of recreation opportunities, not the least of which is fishing. Rafting, hiking, bird-watching, and mountain biking are also popular in this region. Be sure to visit Black Rock and Manby during the late summer or early fall. Other times of the year will be more hazardous and less fulfilling. Roads can be impassable in wet weather, and water levels in the river can be dangerously high. Black Rock, for example, may be totally submerged during high runoff periods. For information contact the Bureau of Land Management (BLM), which administers the Rio Grande Wild and Scenic River Recreation Area; www .blm.gov/programs/national-conservation-lands/new-mexico/rio-grande-wsr; (575) 758-8851.

Ojo Caliente, included in this section, is a destination in and of itself. One of the oldest hot spring resorts in the country, Ojo Caliente offers a variety of attractions and treatments all within a beautiful setting rich in history and lore. It is a perfect way to get away, relax, and enjoy this part of New Mexico's culture.

35. **BLACK ROCK HOT SPRINGS**

General description: This small grouping of hot springs forms a little pool alongside the Rio Grande, open during lower flow periods of the river.

Location: Northern New Mexico, along the upper reaches of the Rio Grande, outside of the town of Arroyo Hondo, approximately 15 miles from Taos

Primitive/developed: Primitive. The only improvement to the springs has been the continual reconstruction of the rock pool that holds the hot spring water.

Best time of year: Late summer and early fall. Roads may be difficult or impassable after heavy rains. During high spring runoff, the pool is inundated with cold river water and occasionally gets completely washed out.

Restrictions: None. The hot springs are located within the BLM's Rio Grande Wild and Scenic River Recreation Area.

Access: The springs are located at the end of a fairly well-maintained dirt road, which may be impassable in wet weather, and a 0.25-mile hike.

Water temperature: The source is approximately 106 degrees, though the pools are cooler as the hot spring water mixes with river water. During summer the main pool is about 98 degrees.

Nearby attractions: Manby Hot Springs; Taos

Services: Gas, food, and lodging can be found in Taos, approximately 15 miles away. The hamlet of Arroyo Hondo offers a small store and lounge.

Camping: There are no camping facilities in the area of the hot springs, but several campgrounds are in other locations in the Rio Grande Wild and Scenic River Recreation Area, as well as the Carson National Forest to the east.

Map: USGS Arroyo Hondo quadrangle (1:24,000 scale)

For more information: Bureau of Land Management, Taos Field Office; www.blm.gov/programs/national -conservation-lands/new-mexico/rio -grande-wsr; (575) 758-8851

Finding the spring: From Taos, travel north out of town on US 64 to the intersection with NM 522 at a traffic light. Stay straight on NM 522 (US 64 goes to the left) and proceed 7 miles to the small town of Arroyo Hondo. Look for CR 005 on the left (west) immediately after crossing a bridge (and north of an old mini mart). Travel west on CR 005 for 0.8 mile, where the pavement ends and the road crosses a small bridge. Stay on the main dirt road as it curves around uphill, traveling for another 0.7 mile to where you bear right on the main road (to the left goes toward houses). Continue for another 1 mile; the road hugs the cliff above Arroyo Creek before descending into the canyon. Stay left crossing a small bridge, until you reach the Rio Grande (2.5 miles from NM 522). Cross the river on the large steel bridge (John Dunn Bridge), and turn left on the other side. Follow this dirt road along the Rio Grande for 0.3 mile to a parking area at a hairpin turn above the river. Park here if there is room, and follow a fairly well-defined trail downhill (upstream) for approximately 0.25 mile. The hot springs can be identifiable by the small pools on the side of the river, visible only when you are right on top of them.

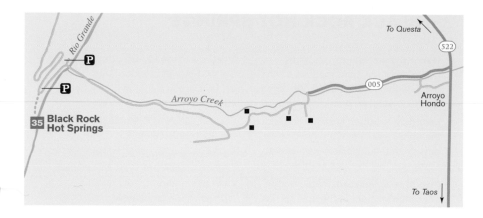

THE HOT SPRINGS

Located along the spectacular canyon of the Rio Grande, Black Rock Hot Springs is a fun place to visit. Also known as Hondo Hot Springs, Black Rock consists of a small collection of hot springs emerging from underneath a pile of large basalt boulders on the banks of the Rio Grande. The water bubbles into one rather large soaking pool, approximately 12 feet in diameter and 4 feet deep. This pool is quite nice, with a sandy bottom and warm temperature (generally 98 degrees). During the winter, and especially during spring runoff, the hot spring water may be inundated by cold river water.

Black Rock's riverside pool is generally lukewarm but always scenic.

The pool itself occasionally gets washed out, too. A cooler pool is located closer to the river, offering a nice bathing option during the hotter periods of summer.

Nudity is not uncommon at Black Rock, though not universal. The best time to visit is generally in the summer and early fall. Roads may also be too difficult during wet winter and spring months. Black Rock is fairly well known and easy to reach, so don't expect to have it to yourself. Just be sure to practice good hot spring etiquette when visiting. In addition to hot spring soaking, there are plenty of fishing opportunities in the Rio Grande as well as on Arroyo Creek, which feeds into the river.

Black Rock Hot Springs, unlike their neighbor, Manby, were never commercially developed. John Dunn purchased the bridge over the river here in 1900, hoping to derive an income from stage service between Taos and the small town of Sevilleta on the railroad. He built a hotel near the bridge, which he understandably used as a stop on his stage line. The stage stopped for the night at the hotel, forcing passengers to pay for lodging and food at Dunn's establishment. Though he desired to exploit the hot springs nearby, their low flow and inaccessibility prevented him from doing so. Dunn's stage line and hotel were never very successful and were short-lived. Little remains today.

36. MANBY HOT SPRINGS

General description: A fabulous grouping of hot springs bubbles into several rock-lined pools along an undeveloped portion of the Rio Grande Gorge.

Location: Northern New Mexico, along the upper Rio Grande, approximately 12 miles from Taos

Primitive/developed: Primitive. Though the springs were at one time part of a short-lived resort, there are only ruins and makeshift rock tubs today.

Best time of year: Summer and early fall. Roads may be too muddy in winter and spring, and pools may be washed out during high river levels (generally early March to late May).

Restrictions: None. The hot springs are located within the BLM's Rio Grande Wild and Scenic River Recreation Area.

Access: A little over 4-mile drive on a dirt road is required, along with a 0.5-mile hike down a steep trail. Though generally well maintained, the road may be impassable in wet weather.

Water temperature: The source is approximately 100 degrees, though the pools are somewhat cooler and vary in temperature.

Nearby attractions: Black Rock Hot Springs; Taos

Services: Gas, food, and lodging can be found in Taos, approximately 12 miles away.

Camping: There are no developed camping facilities at the springs, but there are no restrictions against camping nearby. There are several developed campgrounds in the Rio Grande Wild and Scenic River Recreation Area as well as the Carson National Forest. Be sure to check with the BLM for all the latest restrictions.

Map: USGS Arroyo Hondo quadrangle (1:24,000 scale)

For more information: Bureau of Land Management, Taos Field Office; www.blm.gov/programs/national -conservation-lands/new-mexico/rio -grande-wsr; (575) 758-8851

Finding the spring: From Taos, travel north on US 64 for 4 miles to the intersection with NM 522 at a traffic signal. Turn left (west) here, following US 64, and drive approximately 4 miles to Tune Drive on your right (north). Tune Drive is a graded dirt road, and is approximately 0.3 mile past the airport, which is on your left. Coming from the west, Tune Drive is 23.5 miles from Tres Piedras. Drive on Tune Drive for approximately 4.6 miles, staying on the main road. There are many private driveways and smaller dirt roads leading off from Tune; just stay on the main road. At about 4 miles in, bear left onto a lesser-maintained dirt road (the other road has a sign for Dobson's). Follow the signs for Manby to a broad unmarked parking area overlooking the Rio Grande Gorge. Park in the lower portion, and follow a trail at the left (downstream) side of the parking area to the river for about 0.5 mile, descending 400 feet. You will see the hot springs at the end of the trail at the river.

In the event access via Tune Road is blocked, an alternative, though much more difficult, route is also available. From Taos, drive north on US 64 to NM 522 at a traffic light, and continue straight on NM 522. After 5.3 miles look for CR B007 and turn left. Drive for 2.3 miles on this well-maintained dirt road to a poorly maintained road on your left. Turn here and drive 0.5 mile, where you bear left, then right at 0.7 mile. Travel for another 0.5 mile, staying on the main road to the parking area (1.8 miles from where you split from CR B007). This road is not well maintained and will be impassable after wet weather. Four-wheel drive is recommended at all times.

THE HOT SPRINGS

Also known as Stagecoach Hot Springs, Manby is a fantastic place to visit. Consisting of several hot spring sources, at one time it was the location of a stage station and bathhouse. As with all the other hot springs in the state, Manby was first used and enjoyed by Native Americans. They were well known to the Puebloan peoples of the Taos region, which brought the attention of Spanish explorers in search of the fabled fountain of youth. Although the Spanish visited the springs, it wasn't until the late nineteenth century that Euro-Americans began to exploit the location.

A well-worn footpath leading down to the springs was used by Native Americans and Taos residents for centuries for bathing and washing clothes. In the 1890s a couple of entrepreneurs from Taos decided to build a road that would connect their community with the Denver & Rio Grande Railroad at Tres Piedras. To do this, the two men constructed a toll road across the Rio Grande Gorge, building a bridge just downstream of the hot springs. The road had to be cut into switchbacks on both banks of the gorge. For several years prior to the rise of the automobile, a stage line traversed the route that stopped at the springs.

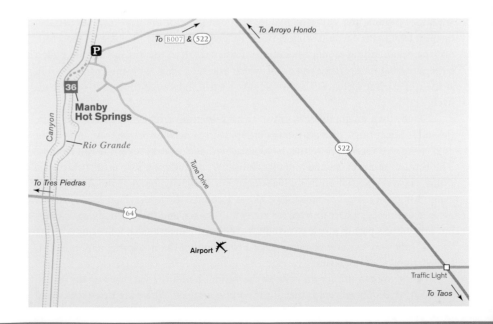

The largest pool at Manby Hot Springs provides the best bathing.

In 1906 a fascinating character by the name of Arthur Manby acquired property that encompassed the hot springs and decided to put it to good use. Manby was an immigrant from England, having arrived in New Mexico in 1882. He soon thereafter began to acquire land in the Taos area, much of it through shady dealings. Through what many would call swindles, Manby obtained most of the land from an original Spanish land grant encompassing close to 100,000 acres. Once he obtained the property, he began raising money to develop a luxury resort at the hot springs. He built a large stone bathhouse, the remains of which you see today, with the entrance a full story over the hot spring. Guests would take a small staircase into the hot-water bath itself.

Manby then sought to draw visitors to his resort, advertising the curative properties of his hot springs, primarily to easterners who came west on the train. A flood in 1927 destroyed several cabins that he built, as well as the bridge over the Rio Grande. The bathhouse never became popular, however, and Manby was unable to turn a profit. He was found dead in his Taos home in 1929, decapitated, and local legend claims his ghost roams the area today. Other accounts, however, claim Manby in fact escaped to Europe, where he lived for many more years, and that the body was not his but instead was part of a ruse to avoid his creditors. Nevertheless, following Manby, various other owners attempted to make a profit out of the hot spring and its resort, though none were successful.

Today you can still see the ruins of the various buildings that made up the resort. The most well-defined ruin is that of the bathhouse itself. There are three rock-lined pools to choose from, each with a sandy bottom. The main bathing opportunity consists of a large rock-lined pool at the edge of the river, several feet deep and wide, with a temperature of approximately 98 degrees. It does, however, get washed out periodically. A slightly warmer bath lies at the foot of the old stagecoach station, provided it is not also washed out. Other small pools can be found along the river, also during dry weather.

This is a great location, with the mighty Rio Grande in the background and the old stage road visible on the other bank. The trail you follow down to the hot springs is, in fact, a part of the old stage road, and if you look closely, you can see retaining walls built into the hillside. Manby is a well-known spring, but you can still find relative seclusion here during the week. There have been numerous reports of car break-ins at the trailhead, so be sure to bring all valuables with you. Please carry out all your trash, stay out of the historic structures, and do not touch any petroglyphs you may encounter.

With increased notoriety, the hot springs have caused some headaches for neighbors living along Tune Drive. The sheer volume of traffic is more than the road can handle, and has led to deterioration and an increased cost to maintain it. This cost is borne by the residents along the road. There has been some talk of closing this road to the public, but this appears to be a last resort at this point. Please be respectful of the road, the land, and the private property along the route to the springs.

37. OJO CALIENTE MINERAL SPRINGS RESORT & SPA

General description: This thriving mineral springs spa and resort has a long tradition and lots of history. Ojo Caliente has become a lush spa resort with many upgrades and improvements.

Location: Northern New Mexico, between Taos and Santa Fe

Primitive/developed: Developed

Best time of year: Year-round

Restrictions: Ojo Caliente is a private resort open for day use and overnight guests. Reservations are recommended.

Access: The resort is located immediately off a highway.

Water temperature: There are several sources for the mineral springs, ranging from 80 to 106 degrees. Temperatures in the baths vary from 85 to 106 degrees.

Nearby attractions: Taos; Santa Fe; Carson National Forest

Services: There are a variety of lodging choices at Ojo Caliente, along with a full restaurant. Gas, food, and lodging can be found in the town of Ojo Caliente itself, immediately adjacent to the resort.

Camping: There is an RV park, along with several tent camping sites, immediately adjacent to the resort.

Map: New Mexico state highway map

For more information: Ojo Caliente Mineral Springs Resort & Spa; www.ojospa.com; (505) 853-2233

Finding the spring: From Taos, travel north on US 64 for 4 miles to the intersection with NM 522 at a traffic signal. Turn left (west) here, following US 64 for 27 miles to Tres Piedras. Turn left (south) on US 285 and travel 30 miles to Ojo Caliente. From Santa Fe, travel north on US 285 for 24 miles to US 84 in Española. Turn west (left) on US 84/285 and continue for 6 miles to Hernandez. Turn north (right) here onto US 285 and drive another 18 miles to the town of Ojo Caliente. Once there, keep an eye out for a sign for Ojo Caliente Mineral Springs, and follow a small street to the resort.

THE HOT SPRINGS

Rich in history, Ojo Caliente was enjoyed by countless generations before there was a resort here. The resort, however, is one of the oldest continuously operating in the country, and offers a variety of baths and treatments. Ojo Caliente is indeed unique, and just the place to come for relaxation. It offers several outdoor pools of varying temperatures, private individual tubs, and a variety of therapeutic treatments including massages, wraps, facials, and mud baths. The high mineral content of Ojo Caliente has been lauded by those who partake of the springs, the waters of which are derived from a massive volcanic aquifer that produces more than 100,000 gallons per day. Today, the resort is a part of a larger spa consortium that includes a second spa in Santa Fe known as Sunrise Springs. While Ojo Caliente has certainly "matured" over the past twenty years into a more lavish resort than it once was, it's still a great place to visit.

Each of the new private pools at Ojo Caliente comes with a small courtyard and fireplace.

Native Americans enjoyed the springs for generations before the Spanish knew of their existence. A group of Puebloan people (ancestors of the Tewa) considered the springs sacred, believing them to be an opening to the underworld. They built a village overlooking the springs and called it Posi, or Poseuinge, "village at the place of the green bubbling hot springs." The village contained numerous structures, housing well over 1,000 people, but according to oral history tradition was abandoned sometime in the sixteenth century after an epidemic. Other Native American groups used the springs thereafter, including such distant tribes as the Ute, Comanche, and Navajo. Interestingly, tradition states that the springs were a sort of neutral ground between these groups, who often otherwise fought.

Spanish explorer Alvar Nuñez Cabeza de Vaca visited the site in the mid-sixteenth century and was amazed by the springs, naming them Ojo Caliente. By the early nineteenth century, Spanish settlers had carved out a small community in the valley near the hot springs, despite continued raids by Utes and Comanches. The village became known as Ojo Caliente and gained fame the world over.

In 1880 the hot springs were developed into a resort by Antonio Joseph, and beginning in 1881, could be reached from the Denver & Rio Grande Railroad via a 10-mile stage ride. Lodging was available, along with a post office and general store (where Kit Carson is said to have traded). The bathhouse that stands today was built during this period, and many of the springs were dug out considerably, providing additional bathing opportunities. In 1916 a large hotel building (which still stands today) was constructed, and in 1924 a round adobe barn (which has recently been restored) was built to house dairy cows that supplied the resort. By 1932 the Mauro family acquired the resort, and operated it for the next several decades. New owners came along in 1999 and have completed numerous upgrades while honoring the history of the resort. The resort has certainly developed past its rustic feel, though some of that feeling can still be had in the historic hotel.

The focus at Ojo Caliente is the natural mineral water and its role in providing a relaxing environment for guests. For generations people have believed in the curative properties of Ojo Caliente's mineral waters, and its current owners and guests continue to do so today.

There are now seven pools to choose from, with more on the way. The focus of the pool area is the historic adobe bathhouse, built in the 1880s. Outside the bathhouse is a seasonal mud pool (May to October); inside are steam and sauna rooms, and several private mineral tubs. Adjacent to the bathhouse are the four main pools (both indoor and outdoor), consisting of the Lithia Spring, Iron Spring, Arsenic Spring, and Soda Spring. Each of these unique pools is of a different temperature, and each possesses its own curative claims. You can also enjoy the Kiva Pool as well as the Mud Pool (where mud can be applied to the skin if you so choose).

Steam and sauna rooms are also available in the bathhouse; bathing suits are required in these public areas. Three newer private baths are immediately adjacent to the main pool area, and bathing suits are optional in them. A per-person fee is charged for use of all of the mineral pools, steam rooms, saunas, and mud pool. Fees are charged for use of the private outdoor baths for twelve minutes each. The baths are open from 9:30 a.m. to 10 p.m. daily.

Accommodations are provided in the historic hotel building as well as in a variety of other room types. In the historic hotel, there are no showers or bathtubs in the rooms, as traditionally all bathing is done in the bathhouse. All other rooms, however, have full baths, and some come with their own private hot spring pool. There are also two private houses available, the Adobe and the Casa de Ojo, providing every kind of amenity needed. Lodging rates vary for use of the small hotel rooms and private homes. Overnight guests receive full access to the mineral pools each day. A full restaurant offers breakfast, lunch, and dinner.

38. PONCE DE LEON HOT SPRINGS (TAOS PUEBLO TRIBAL HOT SPRINGS)

General description: A former resort long since demolished still offers a rustic bathing experience after a short walk. Closed for many years, the springs were recently transferred to the Taos Pueblo tribe, which has allowed access again.

Location: Near the town of Taos

Primitive/developed: Primitive. This is a long-abandoned resort, with only the foundations of the buildings remaining, though the pools themselves remain.

Best time of year: Year-round

Restrictions: The hot springs are owned and managed by the Taos Pueblo. Restrictions include day use only and no motor vehicles, fires, camping, or pets in the pool.

Access: The hot springs require a hike of approximately 1 mile to reach.

Nearby attractions: Taos

Services: None

Map: USGS Ranchos De Taos quadrangle (1:24,000 scale)

For more information: Taos Pueblo; (575) 758-1028; taospueblo.com

Finding the spring: From Taos, take NM 68 south to Ranchos de Taos. Turn left on NM 382 (Llano Quemado Road). Follow this road for approximately 2.2 miles; the main road will soon turn to dirt. This is Miranda Canyon Road. As the road bends to the left at a fork, you will see the gate across the road on the right. There will be signs for the hot springs. Park here, cross under/around the gate, and follow the road for approximately 1 mile to the hot springs. The trail crosses over a small creek, which is the old *acequia* or drainage canal. You will then come to the ruins of the old swimming pool, which no longer holds water. Continue along the path and you will reach the bathable pools.

THE HOT SPRINGS

Ponce de Leon Hot Springs, also known as Taos Pueblo Tribal Hot Springs, has gone through many iterations since its founding many years ago as a resort. After its abandonment and demolition of the structures, the hot springs became a party spot. Due to abuse and a variety of problems, the hot springs were closed for many years. Recently, they were acquired by the Taos Pueblo tribe, which has cleaned them up and allowed access again. The hot springs consist of a variety of concrete pools from the former resort. There is one main swimming pool, where the water is generally in the low 90s, along with several other smaller pools adjacent. It appears clothing is optional. Be sure to respect this place and do your part to ensure it stays open for public use. There is a fenced-in area that encloses a pool for use by tribal members only.

Ponce de Leon Hot Springs was a part of the Cristóbal de la Serna Land Grant, which was established in 1710, and was situated next to the Camino Real. Prior to that, of course, the hot springs were sacred to the people of Taos Pueblo, as well as to the Picuris Pueblo. The hot springs water was used in irrigation for centuries by nearby farmers in the Llano Quemado area.

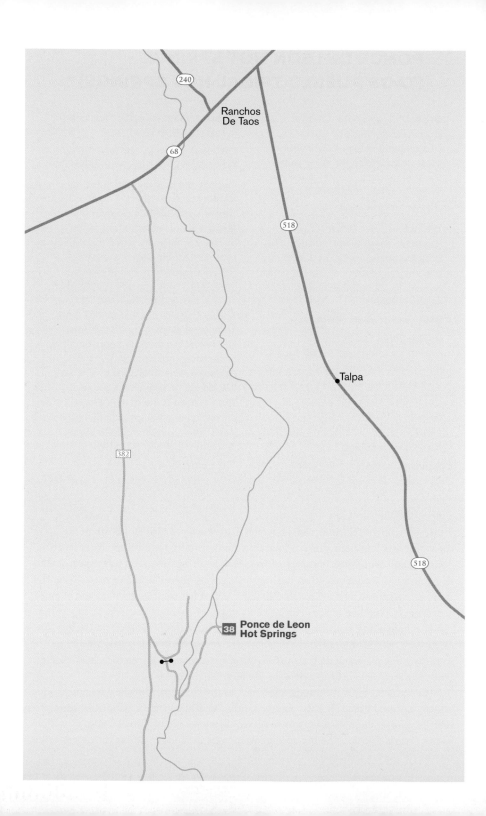

A small resort was created in the late 1920s by the Martinez Family. The concrete pools that you see today were built at this time. By the 1960s, however, hippies had "discovered" the Taos area, including Ponce de Leon Hot Springs. The hot springs and the entire area in general were soon overrun, and clashes with locals were inevitable. In 1973, the Río del Norte Development Corporation purchased the property, with plans to build a new resort. These plans were never realized, however, and the land was sold to the Miranda Limited Partnership in 1992. The Taos Land Trust purchased the property in 1997, with financial assistance from an anonymous donor, to protect it from future development. Finally, in 2016, the property was transferred to Taos Pueblo, which now provides access under limited circumstances. These include "supervised educational programs, nature observation, ecological and geological study, and non-motorized pedestrian recreation."

APPENDIX A: FURTHER READING

Back, William, Edward R. Landa, and Lisa Meeks. "Bottled Water, Spas, and Early Years of Water Chemistry." US Geological Survey Groundwater 33 (July–August 1995): 605–14.

Kammer, David. National Register of Historic Places Registration Form, The Hot Springs Bathhouse and Commercial Historic District in Truth or Consequences, Sierra County, New Mexico. 2004.

Mariner, R. H., T. S. Presser, and W. C. Evans. "Chemical, Isotopic, and Gas Compositions of Selected Thermal Springs in Arizona, New Mexico, and Utah." U.S. Geological Survey Open-File Report 77-654, 1977.

Waring, Gerald A. "Thermal Springs of the United States and Other Countries of the World—A Summary." US Geological Survey Professional Paper 492, 1965.

APPENDIX B:
FOR MORE INFORMATION

US Bureau of Land Management (BLM)
Taos Field Office
226 Cruz Alta Rd.
Taos, NM 87571-5983
(575) 758-8851
www.blm.gov/programs/national
-conservation-lands/new-mexico/
rio-grande-wsr

USDA Forest Service
Carson National Forest
208 Cruz Alta Rd.
Taos, NM 87571
(575) 758-6200
www.fs.fed.us/r3/carson

Gila National Forest, Glenwood Ranger
District
PO Box 8
Glenwood, NM 88039
(575) 539-2481
www.fs.usda.gov/detail/gila/
about-forest/districts/?cid=fse_006122

Gila National Forest, Reserve Ranger
Station
PO Box 170
Reserve, NM 87830
(575) 533-6232
www.fs.usda.gov/detail/gila/
about-forest/?cid=fse_006124

Gila National Forest, Silver City Ranger
District
3005 East Camino del Bosque
Silver City, NM 88061
(575) 388-8201
www.fs.fed.us/r3/gila/about/distmain
.asp?district=silver

Gila National Forest, Wilderness Ranger
District
HC 68, Box 50
Mimbres, NM 88049
(575) 536-2250
www.fs.usda.gov/gila

Santa Fe National Forest
Jemez Ranger District
PO Box 150
Jemez Springs, NM 87025
(575) 829-3535
www.fs.usda.gov/santafe

National Park Service
Gila Visitor Center
Gila Cliff Dwellings National
Monument
HC 68, Box 100
Silver City, NM 88061
(575) 536-9461
www.nps.gov/gicl

PRIVATE HOT SPRINGS
Armand Hammer United World College
of the American West
(Montezuma Hot Springs)
PO Box 248
Montezuma, NM 87731
(505) 454-4200
www.uwc-usa.org

Artesian Bathhouse and RV Park
312 Marr St.
Truth or Consequences, NM 87901
(575) 894-2684

Charles Motel and Spa
601 N. Broadway St.
Truth or Consequences, NM 87901
(575) 894-7154
charlesspa.com

Faywood Hot Springs
165 NM 61
HC 71, Box 1240
Faywood, NM 88034
(575) 536-9663
faywood.com

Fire Water Lodge
311 N. Broadway St.
Truth or Consequences, NM 87901
(575) 740-0315
firewaterlodge.com

Jemez Hot Springs (formerly Giggling
Springs)
40 Abousleman Loop
PO Box 60
Jemez Springs, NM 87025
(575) 829-9175
gigglingsprings.com

Gila Hot Springs Ranch
Route 11, Box 80
Silver City, NM 88061
(575) 536-9314
gilahotspringsranch.com

La Paloma Too Hot Springs (formerly
Hay-Yo-Kay Hot Springs)
300 Austin Ave.
Truth or Consequences, NM 87901
(575) 894-2228
lapalomahotspringsandspa.com/en-us/
baths

Indian Springs
218 Austin St.
Truth or Consequences, NM 87901
(575) 894-2018

Jemez Springs Bath House
062 Jemez Springs Plaza
Jemez Springs, NM 87025
(575) 829-3303
(866) 204-8303
jemezspringsbathhouse.com

La Paloma Hot Springs
311 Marr St.
Truth or Consequences, NM 87901
(575) 894-3148
lapalomahotspringsandspa.com/en-us

Ojo Caliente Mineral Springs Resort &
Spa
PO Box 68
Ojo Caliente, NM 87549
(888) 939-0007, (575) 583-2233
ojocaliente.ojospa.com

Pelican Spa
306 S. Pershing St.
Truth or Consequences, NM 87901
(575) 894-0055
pelican-spa.com

Riverbend Hot Springs
100 Austin St.
Truth or Consequences, NM 87901
(575) 894-7625
nmhotsprings.com

Sierra Grande
501 McAdoo St.
Truth or Consequences, NM 87901
(877) 288-7637
sierragrandelodge.com

Sundial Springs
PO Box 157
Glenwood, NM 88039
(575) 539-2712
sundialsprings.com

Ten Thousand Waves
3451 Hyde Park Rd.
PO Box 10200
Santa Fe, NM 87504
(505) 982-9304
tenthousandwaves.com

The Wilderness Lodge
HC 68, Box 85
Silver City, NM 88061
(575) 536-9749
gilahot.com

Truth or Consequences and Sierra
County Recreation and Tourism
301 S. Foch St.
Truth or Consequences, NM 87901
(575) 894-1968
sierracountynewmexico.info/
truth-or-consequences

Wildwood Retreat
HC 68, Box 79X
Silver City, NM 88061
(575) 536-3600
wildwoodhotspringsretreat.com/index
.html

INDEX

Artesian Bath House and RV Park, 63

Black Rock Hot Springs, 97

Blackstone Hotsprings, 69

Brock Canyon Hot Springs, 41

Charles Motel and Spa, 53

Faywood Hot Springs, 13

Fire Water Lodge, 55

Frisco Box Hot Springs, 9

Gila Hot Springs RV Park and Campground, 27

Gila Hot Springs, 21

Hoosier Hot Springs, 68

Indian Springs, 59

Jemez Hot Springs (Giggling Springs), 86

Jemez Springs Bath House, 83

Jordan Hot Springs, 31

La Paloma Hot Springs & Spa, 61

La Paloma Too Hot Springs (Hay-Yo-Kay Hot Springs), 57

Manby Hot Springs, 100

McCauley Hot Springs, 76

Meadows Warm Springs, The, 35

Melanie Hot Springs, 18

Middle Fork (Lightfeather) Hot Springs, 28

Montezuma Hot Springs, 93

Ojo Caliente Mineral Springs Resort & Spa, 104

Pelican Spa, 64

Ponce de Leon Hot Springs (Taos Pueblo Tribal Hot Springs), 107

Radium Springs, 46

Riverbend Hot Springs, 50

San Antonio Hot Springs, 78

San Francisco Hot Springs, 3

Sierra Grande, 66

Soda Dam, 81

Spence Hot Springs, 73

Sundial Springs, 7

Ten Thousand Waves, 90

Turkey Creek Hot Springs, 37

Wilderness Lodge, The, 25

Wildwood Retreat and Hot Springs, 23

ABOUT THE AUTHOR

Matt C. Bischoff is a historian by trade. He greatly enjoys the wide open spaces and spectacular scenery of the Southwest. Growing up in the West, Matt has lived throughout California, Nevada, and Arizona, and now makes his home in Monterey, California.

Hot springs have always fascinated Matt, and seeking out new ones is one of his favorite pastimes. He has explored the Southwest extensively for this book, as well as for his job, and feels the hot springs described herein are some of the best in New Mexico. He is also the author of *Touring California and Nevada Hot Springs* and *Touring Arizona Hot Springs*, both published by FalconGuides.